The Dharma of History

Liam Martin was born on the Caribbean island of Grenada. He immigrated to the United States in 1978 at the age of seventeen. He has lived in New York ever since, and is a former student of the State University of New York at Stony Brook.

Liam Martin

The Dharma of History

A West Indian Buddhism

GULLY PRESS • New York

Gully Press, 846 Utica Ave., Suite 358, Brooklyn, NY 11203
© 1996 by Liam Martin
Published 1996
Printed in the United States of America

International Standard Book Number: 0-9650892-0-7 Pbk.

Library of Congress Catalog Card Number: 96-94058

Acknowledgment is made to the following for permission to quote material:

BUDDHIST PUBLICATION SOCIETY: From *The Word of the Buddha,* by Nyanatiloka. Former publisher: SASANADHARA KANTHA SAMATIYA. Reprinted by permission of Buddhist Publication Society.
————: From *An Anthology from the Samyutta Nikaya: Pt. 1–3,* Part I, 1981, trans. John Ireland; Part II, 1972, trans. Bhikkhu Nanananda; Part III, 1985, trans. M. O' C. Walshe. Reprinted by permission of Buddhist Publication Society.

WISDOM PUBLICATIONS: From *The Middle Length Discourses of the Buddha: A New Translation of the Majjhima Nikaya,* trans. Bhikkhu Nanamoli and Bhikkhu Bodhi. © Bhikkhu Bodhi, 1995. Reprinted by permission of Wisdom Publications.

PALI TEXT SOCIETY: From *The Rhinoceros Horn and other early Buddhist poems: Sutta Nipata,* trans. K. R. Norman. © Pali Text Society, 1984. Reprinted by permission of the Pali Text Society.

∞ The paper used in this publication meets the minimum requirements of the American National Standard for Information Sciences—Permanence of Paper for Printed Library Materials, ANSI Z39.48-1984.

To my mother and father,
sister and brothers

Long have I searched for that logic
which would lock our hearts into reason.
Never again to be dismayed,
the logic of Dharma I have found.
And I declare: In the Aryan
there is no moral defect.

Contents

Preface

In this book a West Indian experience takes recourse in the language of Buddhism. The appropriateness of this lies in the similarities between the ancient Indian society of early Buddhism and the present West Indian society. Both societies were created from the intermingling of northern Caucasian and darker southern races. We will show that Hinduism and Buddhism—the two major religions of ancient India—were direct responses to the conflicts that arose with the Aryan migrations into ancient Dravidian India (1500–1000 B.C.E.).

This response is assumed for the West Indies, the first territories encountered by Europeans in their colonization of the Americas (from 1492 onwards, and named for the India which they had originally set out to reach), and to which were later brought the African slaves, East Indian, Chinese and Portuguese indentured laborers needed to work on the sugar-cane plantations. It is within the inevitable creolization and fusing of these myriad Old World cultures that are found the conditions reflective of the Buddha's own social environment. In particular, ancient India's system of blood classes and clans and later castes is paralleled in the West Indies by the differential ranking of the various racial groups and the creation of the even more volatile ranking of the mulattoes and the other newly mixed types. It is in this crucible of the New World that we have the most valid context for a modern Buddhist expression. The merging of the Buddha's doctrine with this social experience has proved controversial, but this very controversy will explain just why the Buddha's doctrine was so revolutionary in the first place.

The first essay examines the different compacts reached by three West Indians with their own West Indian experience—a nationalist leader, a poet and a novelist. This essay will familiarize the reader with the social dynamics of the region. The second essay takes us back to the Buddha's India (563–483 B.C.E.) where we learn the language of the Buddha's dharma or doctrine. In the third and last essay we apply this language of Buddhism to the phenomenon of racial identity in the modern world—in particular the United States—but specifically from a West Indian perspective.

Though there is a certain logic to the order in which they are presented here, these essays need not be read accordingly. Each is fairly self-contained. The reader interested in the purely Buddhist angle may go directly to the second essay. Those anxious to see the application of the language of Buddhism to a modern context may start with the last essay. Hopefully, though, wherever the reader starts, he or she will be led on by a deepened interest to the others.

Many people have influenced this book. Two who can never be appraised or thanked enough are my mother and father, Jean and Venis Martin. Three others deserve my appreciation here: my brother, John, fellow traveler and sounding board all these years; Alison, for recommending that I read Ayn Rand; and one who, without knowing it herself, was the mirror of my lost heart.

Note on quotations

In the first essay references are made to the works of Derek Walcott. Abbreviations used are: *Another Life (AL), Midsummer (M), Omeros (O)*.

In three instances in the second essay and all but two instances in the third I have produced my own renderings of passages of the Buddhist canon (the *Tripitaka*) even though I am not fluent in the Pali language in which these scriptures are preserved. But because of the radically new perspective on the Buddha's dharma and the large amount of conceptual change that this entailed, it seemed a natural enough thing to do. Such an attempt also suggests a different cultural context into which translations may be done and so hopefully more accurately reflect the original Buddhist environment. I hope the reader will forgive the inevitable pitfalls.

References in the second essay are given in terms of the appropriate collection, its volume and page number or (comprehensively) the discourse number. Example: M I 20, D no. 8; but Sn 190 since the *Sutta Nipata* consists of a single volume, the number referring to the verse division; in order to refer to an entire discourse of the *Samyutta Nikaya,* a chapter designation (in lowercase Roman numerals) replaces the volume designation, e.g. S ch. xi no. 20. The abbreviations of the various collections are *Samyutta Nikaya* (S), *Majjhima Nikaya* (M), *Digha Nikaya* (D) and *Sutta Nipata* (Sn). References are to the Pali Text Society's versions of the Theravada canon.

Nearly all of the specifically Buddhist words, originally from the Pali and Sanskrit, are given in their English language adaptations. These may be found in the glossary on page 143 or in a good unabridged English dictionary.

Words and concepts that are emphasized, or are 'quoted' from another context, are enclosed in single quotation marks. Double quotation marks always enclose quotations taken directly from textual sources, or denote rhetorical speech.

I
Historical Vision and the West Indian

The modern West Indies are largely the product of three Old World cultures. Following Columbus' crossing of the Atlantic, the Europeans as early as 1520 brought in African slaves to replace the quickly depleted Amerindian conscript labor. After slavery was abolished in the mid-nineteenth century, East Indians were brought in to replace a now reluctant African labor force. In its adopted home each heritage underwent significant change. The African lost all vestiges of an original culture and language. The European retained both language and culture but largely lost its homogeneous bloodline. And the East Indian—though the last to arrive— struggles to retain all of these.

In response to these new conditions of existence, each heritage has produced a major chronicler of its *Zeitgeist* and character. The first was Jamaica's Marcus (Mosiah) Garvey who preached an African nationalism in the first half of the twentieth century. The European and East Indian perspectives have found their most definitive expressions in the careers of two present writers. Derek (Alton) Walcott is a St. Lucian born poet and playwright of mixed European and African heritage. And V. S. (Vidiadhar Surajprasad) Naipaul is a Trinidadian born novelist and travel writer of East Indian descent. The ideas and works of these three figures—each from his particular vantage point—have captured unforgettably the polyglot experience of the West Indies.

The Dharma of History

The ethnocentric legacy of Marcus Garvey

Before European colonization the majority of Africans did not
have a view of themselves beyond their tribal identities. Even the
word 'African' is European, from the Latin *Afer.* The word
'Ethiopian'—which blacks have often seen as a truer identity for
themselves—is derived from the Greek *Aithíops* which refers to
the racial feature of a dark skin complexion which struck Europeans as so very strange. So that even Africa's very identity has
been a creation of Europe from the earliest.

It is untenable that a people would choose to call themselves by
a feature which they all possess, which can in no way be viewed
as strange by them. But this is exactly what a dark complexion
was to the ancient Greeks and Romans; and even in modern times
to the Portuguese and Spanish who were startled by the incongruity of richly melanic complexion and so bestowed the term *negro,*
which denotes the color 'black' in their language. Rebelling
against this alienated valuation of themselves, many have insisted
on replacing this Spanish and Portuguese term with its Anglo-
Saxon equivalent, 'black.' More lately they have sought to replace
this with the very ancient, Latin-derived term 'African.' This, no
doubt, is done in the hope of invoking the classicism of ancient
Rome, and to escape the association with slavery which the term
negro is contemporaneous with. But also in the hope of reclaiming
a solidarity with the African continent and peoples severed by
slavery. Ironically though, both terms 'African' and 'Ethiopian'
originally would have referred to the indigenous Caucasoids of
North Africa (Berber and Egyptian) and East Africa (Cushitic).
For unlike the Portuguese and Spanish, the Romans and Greeks
confronted overwhelmingly Caucasian populations. Though, of
course, to these ancient peoples such names would still have
meant an alienated vision. So both terms 'African' and 'Ethiopian'
—adopted by the black populations originally taken from south of
the Sahara—proceeded from and referred to Caucasian racial
types.

It is indeed remarkable that after more than a century and a half of freedom, the former slaves of the New World have been content to base their identity upon a racial feature, that they have found or produced no cultural achievement to embody an identity in, that they have been satisfied with such an unsophisticated, even primitive form of identity. And when they have sought to seek an identity through geographical origin as Africans (certainly admirable) their recourse is only to a foreigner's vision, still an alienated valuation; recourse only to other men's histories, other men's books, side glances, as it were. In the Semitic Bible they find: "Princes shall come out of Egypt, and Ethiopia shall stretch forth her hands to God"; "Ethiopia, where the gods love to be": which they, with the starved eagerness of children, embrace as wholesome, oblivious to the Caucasian and Semitic character and heritage of their beloved Ethiopia and Egypt.

The harsh truth is that there is no significant continuity between any historical society—that is, any major civilizing movement— and modern sub-Saharan Africans. The present northern European civilization can, through the validity of racial type, seek a continuity in the ancient civilizations of Greece and Rome. Not so the African with Egypt. When he looks to Egypt he finds the Arab, an alien racial type which has inherited Egypt's past for the last millennium and a half; and before that, for another millennium, by other alien types, European Greeks and Romans. And whose modern counterparts, the northern Europeans—English, French and German—are the true heirs of Egypt's intellectual heritage. So even here, modern Africans are cut adrift from their only valid potential link to history.[1]

But it is only upon the recognition of Africa's predominant aboriginal character that a true continental identity can be built, not upon a mythology of past glories. It is only the aboriginal character which has been burnt indelibly into the African soul. This primitive character was retained in the West Indies where Africans were brought by Europeans during the Slave Trade of the seventeenth to nineteenth century. The pervasive poverty, the sparseness and speciousness of education, the factionalism of the individual islands, the very character of the populations, are all inseparable from a preliterate social context. These characteristics are only superficially determined by the disruptive element imposed upon their ancestral societies by European historical society. The West Indies are defined, rather, by the inability of an aboriginal social matrix to support a civilized sensibility—to support a manufacturing sector, civil engineering, and a historical awareness through a system of education. Yet, in this century there has been no shortage of historical visions proposed by West Indians.

The first major historical vision to come out of the West Indies was that of Marcus Garvey (1887–1940). Born to the aboriginal heritage of the black masses of Jamaica, Marcus Garvey was a self-educated man. In other words, he was a man captivated by History, consumed by the civilized sensibility. And to this he became acculturated better than most born to it. Single handedly he sought to bring History and civilization to the "Negroes" of the first half of the twentieth century. As he saw correctly, "it was the lack of foresight" of ancestral Africans which was responsible for the plight of the modern African. (Though it must be admitted that Garvey also held the totally opposite view that ancient Africans were the inventors and greatest exemplars of civilization.)[2] When one thinks of it now, one man attempting to civilize a race, his efforts seem preposterous. Preposterous because not even the nation of Abyssinia, civilized for two or more millennia, was able to make any inroads on the rest of the continent: their expansion to the borders of the present-day Ethiopia was largely the instigation of Europeans in the latter half of the nineteenth century.[3] One suspects that Marcus Garvey's endeavors were always thought to be preposterous by the Europeans of America where he concentrated most of his efforts. But in all fairness, Garvey was more instrumental in raising the awareness of Africans to the historical level than centuries of European colonization. He organized his Universal Negro Improvement Association (UNIA) into various

4

departments of civilization, mimicking the modern civilized societies of America and Europe. There were Black Cross Nurses, a Motor Corps, a Black Star-liner shipping company, and even a Provisional President of Africa and various governmental ministers. His was the first of many such movements. The Rastafarians of Jamaica are the more homegrown legacy. The North American legacy is clearly seen in the black Nation of Islam. And many, if not all of the inceptive independence movements on the African continent, are heavily indebted to him.

With Garvey a wholly new and uncharted vision into history was opened up for Africans. The true heirs to this vision would be the Rastafarians of Garvey's native island of Jamaica. What Garvey had claimed for African people on the political level, the Rastafarians would claim for African people on the religious and mythic level—that is, an absolute independence, an absolute reference for all human value. It was Garvey's total conviction in the equality of the African to the rest of humanity—historically, politically and culturally—that would allow the Rastafarians to make the audacious claim of spiritual preeminence for black people. With this new historical awareness the Rastafarians have sought to transform the indigenous aboriginal awareness which pervaded the African element of West Indian society—pocomania, obeah, shango and voodoo.

Nevertheless, Garvey was automatically eclipsed in the pantheon of Rastafarians by the symbolism of Haile Selassie I of Ethiopia (1892–1975) because even though an extraordinary figure, Garvey still admitted a greater than himself in a Christian God and the Bible. The latter the Rastafarians accepted, assimilating Garvey only secondarily to Biblical understanding. Yet, Rastafarians are more truly Garveyites than Rastafarians, for it was Garvey who gave them their historical awareness.

It was Marcus Garvey who turned their eyes to the stage of History. And there they saw a king, Emperor Haile Selassie I of Ethiopia, sitting upon a thrown of History. A Christian nation since the 4th century, Ethiopian legend had enshrined the Biblical story of the queen of Sheba's visit to Israel's king Solomon—Sheba is the Biblical name of *Saba,* an ancient Semitic kingdom in Ethiopia and southwestern Arabia. Preserved in Ethiopia's own scriptural writings, this legend was the reason for the customary titles of Abyssinian and later Ethiopian monarchs. The royal titles of Haile Selassie I, assumed upon his coronation in 1930—King of Kings, Lord of Lords, Mighty Conquering Lion of the Tribe of Judah, Elect of God and Light of the World—convinced the Rastafarians he was the fulfillment of the Biblical Book of Revelations. Haile Selassie, the name assumed on becoming emperor, meant "Power of the Trinity." Ras (prince) Tafari Makonnen were the emperor's precoronation title, personal and family name.

This is the source of the Rastafarians' identity. It is the religious identity of 'Rastafari' which is remarkable, and not the nationalist one of 'Ethiopian.' For the religious identity transcends even the Abyssinians' relabelling of themselves to accommodate the Europeans' fantasies which they accepted from the Christian missionaries they came into contact with starting in the 16th century. The Rastafarians' success lies in the invoking of an identity that ignores racial typesetting, and the remaking of themselves independent of the external valuation of others.

The allegiance of the Rastafarians for Ethiopia is an allegiance to a historical awareness, to a historical society. Ethiopia is the only continuously indigenous historical society on the African continent. The Rastafarians' allegiance is consciously not to the aboriginal societies which proliferate on the continent. When the Rastafarians invoked the divine kingship of Haile Selassie I they asserted for themselves as African people the most fundamental human values. They asserted for black people a full humanity, casting off their age-old debasement.

The divine kingship claim of the Rastafarians rejected the primitive practice of attributing divinity to objects, which the pocomania and shango of their parents did, and instead saw man as the foremost divine object. By concentrating divinity upon a human individual, it was withdrawn from objects and animals; or at least the divinity in these was made subservient to the divine king. This single act freed them of the irrationality of concrete thought—which the divinity of object phenomena is—and gave them that motivation which is the underpinning of civilization.

With their assertion of the divinity of Haile Selassie I, the Rastafarians had discovered the first mechanism of History. Divine kingship is the basis on which all civilizations have raised themselves out of aboriginal status. The attribution of human divinity is the first discipline of civilization, the earliest occurrence of a cultured and civilized character. When humans became the focus of divinity, society underwent a tremendous change. For only then did man feel himself in control of nature, a true lord of creation. Because man was now the source of divinity, the center of the universe and its powers, human society no longer felt itself at the mercy of a capricious nature. This gave to human society the greatest security it had ever known. It also gave to human potential its greatest license, for now all the universe was man's familiar, his plaything. Since man was now the source of the universe's powers, nowhere did there lurk capricious and overwhelming forces. Divine kingship expanded the character of man beyond the narrow concerns of aboriginal society and made it able to embrace historical awareness and produce the arts of civilization—writing, manufacture and architecture.

Yet despite this seminal achievement, Garvey's vision contained a major flaw, one which had the potential to derail its further development beyond the crude practice of the Rastafarians. In devising his ethnocentric History Garvey had unwittingly acquiesced to the European image of himself. He was 'black,' 'Negroid,' 'African,' all of which referred to a racial feature which was only conspicuous to the Europeans. This dissociation of himself, then, became Garvey's identity. And with this racial feature, given in ridicule, Garvey leveled in one fell swoop all of the endless cultural variation of his ancestral continent, just as the Europeans had done. To the Europeans, the cultural variations which had accrued on the continent over millennia were irrelevant. These people were only remarkable in their racial feature of a high melanic skin complexion. From this tenuous basis, then, Garvey proclaimed the innate oneness of hundreds of distinctive societies. Many have followed him.

Garvey had sought to generate cultural and intellectual creativity from the basis of racial similarity. But the purported unity of Europeans—on which such a claim is based—never existed. European civilization, or any other civilization, has nothing to do with racial unity. The Germanic tribes of northern Europe, who are the prime movers of modern civilization, did not possess any unity during their rise. Nor do they possess such unity today. The Franks, the Anglo-Saxons, the Celts, the Slavs, the Germans, all have mutually exclusive identities which are more sacred to each than civilization itself. Garvey's doctrine of racial unity is a rather simple-minded notion. Despite living through the First World War and witnessing the internecine conflict of the various Germanic tribes, he nevertheless continued to believe that it was racial unity which would generate civilization among the Africans.

If one should seek any single cause of northern European civilization, it would have to be the religion of Christianity. For what the Semitic prophet, Jesus, had achieved was a synthesis of the moral and rational basis of civilization. Christianity was a distillation of the wisdom, up till then, of Mediterranean civilization, in a package and on a fundamental level palatable to the Barbarian tribes of northern Europe. Because it was a critique most severely of Jewish civilization it was wholly rejected by the Jews. But it was just what martial Rome needed. The sublime philosophy of Greece had brought civilization to the Romans. Now the Romans, at the limit of military endeavor, eagerly reached out to Christianity. And it was with Christianity that the Barbarians of the north were civilized, whose aboriginal sensibility earlier military conquest had left intact. It was within Christian belief that these Barbarians were able to escape the confines of their primitive traditions to a larger world view. Modern historians often claim that Christianity was the downfall of Roman civilization, and that the period of inception of Christianity in Europe was something of a 'dark age.' Yet this period of Europe's Dark Ages generated a very high level of civilization among the Barbarian tribes where there was none before. Historians who claim otherwise, speak as though their Germanic traditions were an integral part of Roman and Greek civilization. But nothing could be further from the truth. To the civilized Greeks and Romans the Barbarian tribes of the north might well have belonged to another race, so alienated are the civilized and primitive sensibilities.

Within Christianity the various tribes of Europe were able to forge an identity transcending their particular ethnic affiliations, mimicking Jesus' own rejection of a provincial Jewish identity. The identities that were transcended with Christianity were all based on blood; they were 'racial' identities. All things are relative, and in Europe's closed world each tribe had seen itself as 'racially' distinct. In place of these ethnic identities Christianity substituted cultural or historical forms which could foster civilization; the complete opposite to the black or African identity which was proffered by Marcus Garvey and accepted by so many West Indians. Europe's civilizing identity—Christianity—was nonracial, but in its encounter with Africans bequeathed to them a racial identity.

The ethnocentric dimension of Marcus Garvey's vision has the real potential to overwhelm the crude historical awareness of the Rastafarians, and in fact has led many to reject, as 'the colonizer's,' the more refined historical sensibility found in modern civilization. But no matter the criticisms leveled against this vision as the colonizer's (as indeed it is), the fact remains that it is this vision which has been the colonizer's own redemption from his primitive past, which has given him the audacity to be a colonizer, and, in the process, to be conquerors of his own humiliation and racial doubts and to imbue himself with nobility and pride. It is the colonizer's vision—if that is what one chooses to call a historical vision—which alone can redeem the former slaves and colonized from their own deep humiliation. Do these think that the coloniz-er's nobility of aspect existed from time immemorial? Indeed not. It is simply the close association with the achievements of civiliza-tion, an association which he must fight everyday to maintain.

Aboriginal life suffers a dearth of achievement when compared to civilization. Though aboriginals may, among themselves, have a sense of nobility and pride in their racial features, they have no recourse but to feel humiliation and shame in these same features when confronted with civilization in the hands of someone of different racial heritage. It is the untenable nature of aboriginal society which is the cause of the racial shame and humiliation suffered by its members. Otherwise, one would have to postulate some self-evident morality which would refrain civilization from overrunning the world. That is untenable. It is only a historical awareness which allows man to rule his destiny, which conceives of the destruction of the world and its salvation. Only historical awareness holds the fate of the world and its people in its hands. Those who would shrink away from sharing such frightening powers also shrink away from their own nobility.

Historical awareness is a people's greatest treasure. It's occur-rence among any people is a unique and hard won event. And it is upkept only through the greatest vigilance and mindfulness. This so-called colonizer's vision is the key to the domination of the world, the key to the creation of civilization and its preservation. The detractors of this sensibility no doubt place the greatest value on the material products of Western civilization—its machines, its architecture, its engineering—but its first and greatest product, its historical consciousness, they reject vehemently. Yet, here lies the key to their own creation and control of this technology which they are unable to reject. Historical awareness is the first technol-ogy of civilization, the key to all the others. Unable to embrace and nurture this elemental 'technology' their societies are not one hundred or two hundred or even five hundred years behind the modern West. They are not even where the ancient Greeks were twenty-five hundred years ago. Indeed, without this civilized

10

sensibility it makes no sense to attempt to assess levels of attainment relative to civilized societies.

The multiculturalism of Derek Walcott

Marcus Garvey carried out most of his work in the United States of America. There he had sought to impose the West Indian distinction between mulattoes and blacks. This was altogether rejected. Both whites and blacks in the United States had long ago accepted as hard-and-fast rule the notion that any amount of African heritage automatically determined one's racial identity as black. Garvey's view, however, was well founded. The mulatto heritage in the West Indies has a long history. Unlike the blacks, though, the mulattoes would seek a historical awareness through their European heritage. But even unmixed European West Indians were cast out of a European and historical identity and had to make the same effort to find their way back, as can be seen in the writings of the Dominican born novelist Jean Rhys (1894–1979). The mulatto's own struggle has also taken place in the field of literature. Jamaica's H. G. de Lisser (1878–1944), and British Guyana's Edgar Mittelholzer (1909–1965) were the early pioneers of this tradition. These were all novelists, but it was to be a poet who would give this vision its most eloquent expression.

Derek Walcott, born in 1930 on the island of St. Lucia, is a poet of extraordinary ability who offers a multicultural approach to the world of history.[4] Unabashedly colonial, his poetry gives voice to the multicultural heritage and racial ambivalence of the West Indian mulatto. Through the mulatto's Caucasian heritage Walcott has accessed the wider world of history and so freed the West Indian experience from the ethnocentricity of Marcus Garvey.

Walcott's poetry is a mulatto poetry because while emersed in an African social milieu it demands of the reader the most passionate and heartfelt appreciation of a European sensibility. In the poem "Love in the Valley" (from *The Gulf and other Poems,* 1969) the poet's persona recalls its socialization as a white child. Many an avid Walcott reader will be able to do the same, but for the West Indian reader this was an experience which diminished immeasurably and irrevocably an African reality just outside the door.

This European socialization became the great taboo in the wake of Marcus Garvey's ethnocentric legacy. What unnerves Walcott's West Indian detractors is that he stands within a black social context and so eloquently proclaims a Caucasian sensibility. Such a crystallization of the mulatto experience could not have come at a more opportune time, serving as it does to combat the natural antipathy in the North American mindset sweeping the region. Walcott's poetic persona breaks the North American taboo that the mulatto must confine his sensibility to his African bloodline, however immeasurable this was. Or at least that he should be covert in his expression of his Caucasian sensibility. This is revolutionary not only towards the black perspective, but also towards the white, whose dominant culture had rejected the mulatto and decreed that his identity was to be black. Now here was an unapologetic expression of a Caucasian sensibility in a mulatto, truer than the most inbred Caucasian.

It is no surprise, then, that in his long autobiographical poem *Another Life* (1973), the narrator's link to the island's native life is through its quality of pain and suffering. He rarely draws joy from it. The positive for the narrator—happiness and pleasure—comes from the historical world of his European heritage. And so his immersion in this black life is always through self-denial, the giving up of the positive in exchange for pain. Black identity for the persona is synonymous with pain and deprivation.

The child narrator is steeped in European literature, a natural inheritance from his parents. From this height he sees native island life as tribal and African. The paradox is that while the narrator of this poem draws inspiration from the historical world of his European ancestry—here lies the true source of his creativity—in sympathy with the black character of Gregorias he perceives this same world as responsible for the stagnation and nullity of the island's black population. There is a willingness in the narrator to berate the positive in himself to the benefit of the larger society's character. The narrator's socialization in a core historical identity conflicts with the aboriginal character of the African element in the island. This twin heritage will often lead the narrator to sympathize with the primitive heritage at the expense of the historical.

But though the narrator is deeply sympathetic to this ethnic world of blacks, he is nevertheless driven to renounce it in no uncertain terms. It is this which gives to the poet's persona its universal appeal, the extent to which it has been able to renounce racial identity. On the other hand, the great tragedy and failure of the other two major characters—Gregorias and Harry Simmons— are blamed by the narrator on the indulgence by the society at large in an African racial redemption. But from this stultifying ideology Walcott's poetic persona is determined to find its salvation.

In the later poem "The Schooner *Flight*" (from *The Star-Apple Kingdom,* 1977) Walcott gives us the adult world of the West Indian mulatto. The protagonist of this poem is Shabine, who describes himself as having Dutch, English and African heritage. Shabine's predicament is typical of the mulatto. He feels rejected by his European heritage and culture, and harbors anger at this dominant part of himself. But neither does Shabine embrace a black identity. Disgusted with his West Indian society, and his own marginality, he signs on as a seaman on a schooner.

Shabine's conflict is racial. He is ambivalent about his identity. We see this in his pejorative view of himself. Though he can enjoy some distance from the blacks in his society by moving easily among the island's Caucasians, in this larger world he is still unable to assert his equality of identity. This conflict also shows up in his affair with Maria Conception. She is Spanish with all the allure and exoticness of her Latin culture. Shabine is part of a significantly black and English-speaking society, from which (I assume) his wife was chosen. When the *Flight* passes a line of casuarinas along the Barbados coast, Shabine is driven to reflect on the disparity between the classical European identity and its degraded offspring in the Caribbean. This is the poem's most intensely lyrical piece, and we see here that Maria Conception's Caucasian culture has always been Shabine's deepest nature. But Shabine believes his love is "inferior" because he uses a European frame of reference, and is cynical about his ambitions for a mature identity within this frame of reference. He is made to feel guilty of this by his parallel African heritage. And the implication is that his desire for a Caucasian identity is morally untenable.

Shabine's conflict is probably the most explicit and dramatic of the persona's intrinsic dilemma. He is obsessed with Maria Conception, but is torn by his responsibility to his wife and children. This conflict is not superficial. It drives him to the madhouse. On his discharge he laments his displacement in the scheme of things.

When he leaves the island on the schooner *Flight,* he is seeking answers to questions which in the largest sense are questions of identity. And out of his double alienation he forges a poetic vision that transcends both while still remaining quintessentially West Indian. In this poem Walcott has given cosmologic grandeur to the mulatto's racial dilemma, with Shabine asserting a fundamental unity of self. But it is only when the various identities of his racial heritage have been given up that the mulatto Shabine experiences such a moment of transcendence.

In *Another Life* the poet batters unmercifully those West Indians who see their allegiance as singularly committed to an African heritage, that is, to a Garveyite philosophy, the supremacy of things African. But when Walcott returns in the book length *Omeros* (1990) to the role of African heritage in the West Indies he chooses to attribute a wholesome and passionate invocation of this heritage to Achille, a poor, illiterate fisherman. Achille's poverty and illiteracy obviously are endearing, and more easily justifies his strong allegiance to his African heritage. This is unlike those whom Walcott had earlier denounced; they were the educated who helped themselves unpardonably to the educated sensibility made possible by European civilization, those who were, in reality, 'mulattoes' of culture. Walcott seems unable to accept an unwavering allegiance to things African in these. But in *Omeros* (this title is the modern Greek word for Homer) his poetic persona is perfectly comfortable with such a passionate stance in an uneducated fisherman.

In *Omeros,* Walcott's persona uses the European Plunkett as mature double, and the African Achille as its youthful identity. The persona uses both characters to objectify its mixed cultural and racial heritage, breaking up the resultant identity into its two component vectors. The poet can thus examine symbolically the two currents of his identity. This is exemplified in passages where the persona switches between the agony over a failed marriage and the world that Achille inhabits (chs. xlviii/i & xlix/iii). Though the mature persona (at the time of narration) is most sympathetic to this level of island life with its overwhelmingly African echoes, it obviously looks upon this world from the vantage point of a European Plunkett. The poetic persona grants the fullest sympathy to Achille's world, but confers to Plunkett's the greater reality.

The persona's mulatto heritage is resolved into two starkly opposite characters—Major Plunkett and Achille. Both make journeys into the past, searching for meaning to their lives. The first journey we encounter is Plunkett's (Bk. 2), who does historical research into St. Lucia's past where he seeks some deeper connection to the island. Through this character the island's history is revealed to us, a history which, necessarily, is only through European eyes. Plunkett's research ends when he discovers a namesake, an English midshipman, who died in the Battle of the Saints (1782) which saw Admiral Rodney pitted against Compte de Grasse, and which had St. Lucia as part of the loot the British won from the French.

When Achille makes his journey to the past (Bk. 3), he recreates for us the African heritage of St. Lucia. While Plunkett is literate and hails from an educated culture and carries out his search accordingly, Achille is illiterate—he even misspells the name of his canoe—and is able to access the past only through dream or hallucination. It is in such a state of trance—while he is out at sea in his fishing canoe—that we travel with him to Africa where we see how his ancestors lived and witness a raid on his ancestral village, the purpose of which are captives for the European slave ships waiting on the coast. It is no doubt in this raid that Achille's ancestor, Afolabe, is captured and brought to St. Lucia where he ends up working under the British midshipman, Plunkett, who renames him Achille. The modern day Achille also works a while for the modern day Plunkett who owns a pig farm. Despite the lapse of centuries the role each plays has remained the same: the Africans remain menial laborers, the Plunketts overseers.

These two antagonistic halves come together in the mulatto consciousness of Walcott's poetic persona. But do these two divergent streams ever reach a harmonious whole? The poetic persona never rejects either half outright. Through the most touching and convincing sympathy it embraces the African world of Achille and Helen, Hector, Seven Seas, Philoctete and Ma Kilman. It is not, however, as sympathetic to the European world of Plunkett. (This is with the exception of Maude, Plunkett's wife, and Catherine Weldon, the fictional American character the narrator creates as a catharsis for his estrangement from his wife.) Towards Plunkett (ch. liv/i) we witness an outburst of the narrator and a showing up of Plunkett which breaks the long line of sympathy towards this character and seems totally unjustified, as if indeed the narrator was guilty of "envy." And we have already seen how only grudgingly the poetic persona accedes to European civilization (but accedes nonetheless) the center of gravity of the modern world. It is as if to achieve a harmonious whole the persona demands concession only from the European half.

Yet when in the poem "Sainte Lucie" (from *Sea Grapes,* 1976) the poet seeks to recall his earliest language (as a reprieve from Standard English?), he is not referring to some lost African language. It is true to say that the poetic persona does not feel any desire for an African aboriginal identity. What the poet is, in fact, referring to is St. Lucia's earliest historical language, which is French. The island's deepest historical past is not African; it is

French, the original European colonizers. And Walcott's true element is History, not an aboriginal sensibility. The poet may allow characters to long for an African past and identity, as Achille does. But this is an uneducated fisherman, uninitiated in a historical sensibility, seeking a past and identity of equally prehistorical content. When those West Indians who have been initiated into a historical sensibility—educated, in other words— try to displace this European achievement unto an African past, the poet inveighs against them.

Though Walcott's persona is often grudging, it does accept History's utilitarian view. Rather like the Greek historical awareness which was defined by its conflict with Asia Minor's Troy, so, as a West Indian, the person's historical awareness is defined by the conflict of the European enslavement and colonization of Africans. But the truth is that the poet has, from the earliest, found it impossible to reject his European heritage, even with it carrying out the enslavement of Africans. In "Return to D'Ennery; Rain" (from his first commercially produced collection *In A Green Night,* 1962), the poet despairs that he cannot find it in himself to employ his gift of poetry in the service of hatred on behalf of his parallel African heritage.

In *Omeros,* the character of Plunkett is only one half of the persona's identity. Yet it can be argued that it is this half which is the persona's most fundamental identity. It was under a European cosmology that the persona was first acculturated and acquired its system of values, those values which form one's core self and which one may not pervert without destroying, ultimately, one's sense of reality. And though one might argue that this cosmology, being an educated one, must have been acquired after its untutored African double, yet, for someone like Walcott, his education was begun at the cradle. One may even say that this educated frame of reference was his birthright. Yet, this European cosmology was partly orphaned—as the child Walcott was—able to find material form only in the historical remnants of the French and British occupation of the island. The greater materiality of St. Lucia's life was its African population. It was within this alien materiality that the adolescent boy, Walcott, saw his European cosmology taking on gross form. Developmentally, the poetic persona was confronted with an adult black identity after a white childhood.

That this juxtaposition is the root of the persona's great anguish is not disputed. But from this conflict of mixed heritage Walcott has always seen his salvation in History. But in *Omeros,* has Walcott rejected his earlier salvation? His persona admits that the sacred world portrayed in the Homeric classics is irrelevant to West Indians, and so substitutes the African aboriginal world of obeah. Is this the persona's salvation? But isn't this simply the substituting of one metaphoric world for another?

The world of the gods plays as significant a role in *Omeros* as they do in the *Iliad* and *Odyssey.* In *Omeros,* this world is that of Ma Kilman—the sibyl or obeah woman—whose craft brings redemption to Philoctete and even Walcott's persona, the poem's narrator. This primitive world, the African heritage of the slave populations, is invoked as passionately, and with as much acceptance and faith and even credulity as in Homer. Walcott's poetic persona certainly intends for us as readers to believe in the value of this world; or at any rate, to accept that it is credible in its belief.

In *Omeros* Walcott's persona seeks solace in this aboriginal sensibility when pain enters its own historical awareness. The narrator, reeling from the pain of divorce, admits that his pain was one with Philoctete, the fisherman who was wounded on the shin by a boat's anchor (*OM,* p. 245). Both are finally healed by Ma Kilman's magic art. And yet, after the deepest of condolence from this world, the persona can as convincingly assert a disbelief in the efficacy of religion and the sacred. But which religion and which "myth" did the persona become disillusioned with? Obviously from European religion and European myth. The persona has only rejected one religion and myth for another. We may feel in regard to *Omeros,* like Walcott's persona in regard to Homer's *Iliad* and *Odyssey,* that its aboriginal spirituality is totally irrelevant to us.

18

We have to make an added effort to embrace the aboriginal sanctuary which the persona seeks when its modern sensibility is stressed.

The persona's instinctual yearnings for a true historical awareness are continually thwarted by the pull of its African heritage. In a very telling episode in *Omeros,* the poetic persona and its craft (literally and figuratively) are no less than hijacked. The African crew of its ship, while sailing along the Aegean, mutinies and pronounces a curse on the persona's longing for a European sensibility (*OM,* xl). This is the decisive moment in the poem because this is the farthest distance from its West Indian home that the persona gets. From here its journey turns back towards home. And the persona martyrs its desire and craft to its African heritage. Like a true missionary, self-denial is the persona's salvation.

Like Homer's world, the world of Walcott's poetic persona is half historical, half aboriginal. The persona has one foot in either sensibility. It has not succeeded in fully freeing itself of the mesh of aboriginal sentiment. The great sympathy (and even pity) that the persona feels for the African element in its environment proceeds from the deepest ethnic alienation and the privilege this brings. The persona's European sensibility precedes all else, lies at the basis of everything. The persona looks from the balcony of History at an aboriginal landscape. It anxiously walks back and forth from its lofty porch down to the aboriginal terrain, and up again to its high perch. Walcott's poetry gives one a tour through the West Indian experience from the vantage point of a historical awareness. Though, of course, many have looked at the West Indies with the eyes of History, Walcott's poetry and even his historical awareness one may see as indigenous to these islands. In contrast to others (such as the nineteenth century English historian, J. A. Froude) Walcott's historical sensibility is homegrown. So much so, that it often seems to be in danger of being overwhelmed by the aboriginal.

In Walcott's poetry, what is true for the many is not true for the persona. History is the persona's first home. The aboriginal world is a metaphorical one. The aboriginal may be fundamental for a statistical majority in the persona's social environment, but never for the persona as an individual. It might seem that the poet wants us to believe that the aboriginal realm is fundamental and the historical realm one of metaphors. But this is impossible, because the consciousness which moves through the poetry (the persona's consciousness) is always historical. And this historical consciousness is always possessed by an ethnicity alienated from the majority. The poetic persona is highly individualistic; and the poet has been significantly unsuccessful in bringing this poetic persona's great eloquence to his many plays—which necessarily are *communal* in nature. (This is the opposite of Shakespeare's own accomplishment, where the greatest eloquence was achieved in plays while his poetry itself retained many of the constraining poetic conventions of the Elizabethans.)

The conflict of Walcott's poetic persona consists of an early European sensibility with a later African allegiance, an early historical vantage point with a later aboriginal proximity. The persona in the later work *Omeros* has not resolved this conflict. The poet continues to reaffirm both currents equally. Or one might say that the poet does achieve a resolution by transforming conflict into the more palatable notion of diversity. But is this tenable? And what exactly does it entail? For one thing it would mean grafting an African manhood upon a European childhood, accommodating an African identity to a European development. For another, it would mean grafting an aboriginal sensibility upon a historical vision. If one means by this resolution of diversity a diluting of both extremes, a foundering of the historical vision in an aboriginality, then it is not tenable. The historical vision must remain undiluted. It is the only dynamic element. The aboriginal can only be its focus, its sphere of action. This alone can be the resolution of Walcott's poetry and *Omeros,* if we are to perceive in it a positive meaning. It is the historical vision, pure and unchallenged, which is its redeeming element, and the redemption of the aboriginal. Like Gulliver among the little people, this vision soars above the aboriginal landscape of the West Indies. Only this vision is without inertia, only this vision can transform. This is the true treasure, the sight from the balcony of History. Its focus is a matter of mere circumstance. It is the vision alone that saves, the vision alone that rewards.

Marcus Garvey had sought to fit European and civilized forms upon the aboriginal cultural milieu of the Africans. The same process occurs in Walcott's poetry, only through metaphor, and not social organizational forms. Thus Walcott juxtaposes the civilized forms of European architecture upon the primeval topography of the Caribbean (*M* ii). The persona sees through the eyes of history, sifts the surrounding aboriginal world, as it were, through the high net of history. Some have seen this historical matrix as illusory, metaphorical to the persona, and the aboriginal landscape as the first reality. But the poet's inspiration, his muse, is History. His aboriginal landscape takes on significance only with reference to history. One can even say that without the vantage point of History, the aboriginal landscape would be unacceptable to the poet. Yet the poetic persona does not unequivocally recognize this.

The persona often inveighs against the history which is its core sensibility. The aboriginal is so weighted that it has subverted the persona's original self. This is the great conflict the poet depicts, the suppression of individuality to the will of the majority. The great sadness is that the persona believes its original sensibility is merely metaphorical, and hopelessly seeks to replace it with the secondarily achieved aboriginal sensibility and identity of its maturity, a sensibility and identity which are necessarily superfluous. Walcott's poetic persona rejects the Afrocentric identity of its maturity, but yet cannot fully embrace its Caucasian heritage. Its profound kinship with Europe is mitigated in its identification with the ancient and dead civilizations of Greece and Rome, deflected from a full identification with modern European civilization. This compromise fits well, of course, with the persona's mulatto heritage.

Still, Walcott's vision is revolutionary in its West Indian context. Walcott destroyed the provincial world that Marcus Garvey had bequeathed to the West Indies. But Walcott revealed this larger world of history only to denounce it, and to assert its inherently immoral status (*AL,* p. 109). Walcott's poetic persona is unable to enter the world of History guiltless. And so it makes this world morally inferior to Garvey's ethnocentricity, the very ethnocentricity which it supersedes by its mere acknowledgment of the wider world.

We may wish to say that *Omeros* (and Walcott's body of work, in general) captures the West Indian psyche. But which West Indian psyche? Is the deep sympathy expressed for the African presence in the West Indies a valid road for this African element to travel to Walcott's poetic persona's mulatto frame of mind? Can the African element in the West Indies (or anywhere else, for that matter) avail themselves of Walcott's ennobling vision? Or is this vision simply the same old European benevolence towards the natives, to be rejected as a mutilation of an African essential?

It goes without saying that the consciousness which moves through Walcott's poetry is an undiluted mulatto consciousness (multicultural, it is often called) and is just as much unable to pledge full allegiance to a Garveyite ideology of unswerving commitment to things African, as it is to accepting wholeheartedly a European cultural milieu undiluted by African influences. It is only in the gross vision of North Americans that Walcott is designated 'black.' Walcott has enthroned the *mulatto* and imbued his creole vision with as much nobility as many another European tribe, the Anglo-Saxon, the French, the German.

If there is a flaw in Walcott's poetry, it occurs only through misunderstanding. The foreign reader of Walcott is apt to think that the poetic persona's lofty vision, its European historical awareness, is shared indiscriminately by the persona's subjects. Nothing could be further from the truth. The persona's vision is an aristocratic one. In the poem "Homecoming: Anse La Raye" (from *The Gulf and other Poems,* 1969) the persona is reminded once again of its alienation from the island's folk life, and is heart-broken at the gulf that exists between itself and the native children who mistake him for a tourist. The persona resorts to euphemisms. The children would hardly have mistaken him for a tourist just from his "posture" and "clothes." The real reason, which the persona cannot find it in itself to say, but which any West Indian would know, is its fair complexion. A foreign reader would overlook this. One may wonder if it is not the denial of this factor of ethnic distinction which has made foreign critics see Walcott's early work as "overwrought" and as "stilted imitations of English poets." Would the same poetry in their hands be seen as superficial or borrowed?

The persona's allegiance to a European historical awareness, its avowed "exorcism" in its practice, by its own admission are forever denied its beloved subjects. This eternal conflict (or ambidexterity) is the mulatto's heritage. In iss long career, the persona started off in ambivalence at this heritage. But through the three decades since, has succeeded in staking out a place for its hybrid vision, alloyed from its twin heritage, and defending it against all its detractors.

In the final analysis, Walcott's poetic persona cannot be tied down. The poetic medium, especially when used by someone of such phenomenal powers, is simply a medium of expression; it cannot confine itself to any single viewpoint. It ranges everywhere giving expression to every deep feeling, every passion, every pain. Within Walcott one can find the whole of life's experience. His is truly an alphabet of the West Indian cultural experience, a consummate and seaworthy "craft of words." It is the act of poetry itself which transcends all of the persona's conflicts and ambivalence. That is History's first requirement. It is also Walcott's essential function and his undiminished greatness, the forging of a language for a new experience.

Those who seek a new truth in Walcott and think there are too many words, too much rhetoric, they are ignorant of the function of poetry. This function is simply language, the expression of a landscape, a topography, a life-experience. There *is* a new truth in Walcott and it stares the critics in the face. It is the West Indian experience, that hybrid form, as when three millennia ago wave after wave of Aryan migrations swept into northern India and, coupling with the Dravidian experience, gave birth to the hybrid East India, Bharat.

And so Walcott acknowledges as his "master" the one who found the words for Greece, and taught Europe her first History lesson. The value of *Omeros* (and Walcott's body of work, in general) is not the allegiance to the aboriginal world of obeah which the narrative plot has as giving cure to the sore of Philoctete and the emotional pain of the poetic persona. The value of *Omeros* lies in the juxtaposition of the aboriginal sensibility alongside a historical awareness; in the access of the aboriginal to the historical, just the opposite direction to the narrative plot. That was also the function of Homer to the Greeks, the providing of a historical vent for an aboriginal sensibility: from the world of obeah to a world of historical sentiment. So we are perfectly justified in taking Omeros' advice to Walcott's poetic persona to disregard the aboriginal spirituality of the Greek classics and digest the remainder. If we do, we will be led to V. S. Naipaul, since he alone has truly rejected the world of the gods.

V. S. Naipaul's renunciation

The vision of the Trinidadian born novelist V. S. Naipaul (b. 1932) presents the greatest divergence from the ethnocentric legacy of Jamaica's Marcus Garvey. The characteristic feature of Naipaul's writing is renunciation. His protagonists are always leaving, turning their backs upon, giving up, running away from, a Third World sensibility. In *Miguel Street* (1959), Naipaul's first completed work, the teenage narrator is only too relieved to finally leave the island of his birth and childhood, Trinidad, for England. More than twenty years later, with the novel *A Bend in the River*

(1979), Naipaul has achieved in Salim, the narrator/protagonist, the consummate form of this sensibility of renunciation.

But it is in *The Mimic Men* (1967) that we find the seeds of all the conflicts that are resolved in *A Bend in the River*. In *The Mimic Men,* the narrator Ralph Singh first leaves the island of Isabella hoping never to return, but returns only to leave it in such a manner as to preclude any hopes of ever returning. In this novel the narrator is very conscious of his renouncer's role. Singh views his life as having already passed through the first three life stages as prescribed by orthodox Hindu dogma—student, householder and man of affairs—and now at forty years of age arrived at the last stage, that of the renouncer, when the practitioner abandons the world of individual identities to seek in solitude and meditation the universal identity of **Brahma.**

It is this fourth stage of Hindu life (that of the renouncer) which in the sixth century B.C.E. the Buddha and many of his contemporaries would emphasize to such a degree that it would consume their whole lives, no longer being confined to merely the last years of one's life. While still a young man the Buddha abandoned his wife, son and caste role to join the large company of renouncers that had become an integral part of the life of the Gangetic plain. The significance of this phase of India's history is not lost on Naipaul. In a very revealing article "A Plea for Rationality" (collected in *Indians in the Caribbean,* 1987) Naipaul notes that those Indians who were brought to the West Indies came from the same part of India as the Buddha—the society of northern India's Ganges basin.[5]

The character of Naipaul's renunciation (literary or otherwise) mimics that of these ancient renouncers. Here the Anthropologist Michael Carithers describes for us the world and mindset of the renouncers of the Buddha's time, but he might just as well be describing Naipaul's literary vision, so compatible are the two:

They looked upon the society of the Ganges basin as from afar, and disdained it. They were indeed homeless wanderers . . . spiritual strivers

. . . renouncers of the world and its fruits. But they were also perhaps India's only true cosmopolitans, citizens of the whole, not just of part.[6]

This lofty renunciation, though, has cruder origins. As East Indians on the island of Trinidad, Naipaul's family feels the need to distance itself from "Negro" life (*Finding the Center,* 1984).[7] It must have seemed to a young Brahman Naipaul that the degradation and squalor of the many blacks in Trinidad were the larger than life evocation of the world of untouchability that he knew in microcosmic detail in his own community. His insular Indian community also felt besieged by this chaotic world, which lacked the core historical pretensions that they possessed.

From the earliest, Naipaul the writer refused to see any sacredness in reality. This was the Hindu renouncer in Naipaul perceiving the vanity of all human endeavor. Coupled with Naipaul's literary genius, this stark vision first showed itself as a biting laughter. In these early writings Naipaul saw little redeeming qualities in his fellow humans. But it was when Naipaul combined this renouncer's sensibility with a fully conscious acceptance of a European historical vision that we have the explosive writings of *Guerrillas* (1975) and *A Bend in the River* (1979).

This vision of the pervasiveness of suffering and decay and the illusory nature of the world must have captivated the sensitive young Naipaul even before an Anglo-Saxon sensibility could have. And we do have many references to this. Singh, the protagonist of *The Mimic Men,* recounts how as a child he could never immerse himself in the imaginary worlds of English children's books. In the autobiographical *Finding the Center* (1984), Naipaul also gives direct testimony that the European sensibility remained largely incomprehensible to him. Naipaul simply took his formative Indian sensibility and applied it to the surrounding black Trinidadian society. This vision was the characteristic impassioned Indian sensibility of the renouncer.

It is in *The Mimic Men* that a minor character, Eden, contemplates the most intriguing and audacious act of renunciation. The narrator, Singh, notes of Eden that "His deepest wish was for the Negro race to be abolished," but as to this wonders, "How could anyone, wishing only to abolish himself, go beyond a statement of distress?"[8] Eden and Browne, both "Negroes," and another character, the mixed-race boy Hok, are unable to share in Singh's salvation through renunciation. Their turning away (an "abolishment") is never equal to Singh's own turning away of renunciation. For Singh, their African heritage, whether they possess it wholly or in part, starts and ends in distress. It allows no way of escape, no positive center around which freedom can be built.

It is the boyhood character of Hok, I believe, that Naipaul presupposes for the adult character of Jimmy Ahmed in the later novel *Guerrillas.* Both Hok and Jimmy Ahmed are mixed-race with the Negro strain being the minor admixture and the Chinese the greater. And the humiliation that Hok suffers in *The Mimic Men* when his Negro connections are shown up would fit in well, psychologically, with Jimmy Ahmed's identity crisis. In *Guerrillas,* Roach—ethnic English, former freedom fighter, exiled from South Africa—Jimmy Ahmed, and Roach's companion, the English woman Jane, all play out a love/hate relationship with the fictional West Indian island of Isabella. At the end of this novel Roach has played out all possibilities on the island. Jane, even more unlucky, never escapes. And Jimmy Ahmed—like Eden, Browne and Hok of *The Mimic Men*—are further than ever from that Aryan renunciation that was Singh's salvation, trapped in an identity of pathological ambivalence.

Jimmy Ahmed is one of the major West Indian characters in *Guerrillas.* His father is Chinese, his mother a mulatto. Jimmy thus has an overwhelming blood-claim to two of the worlds great historical traditions, Chinese and European, and only secondarily to the aboriginal tradition of his African heritage. And Jimmy has grown up with his Chinese father, a privileged upbringing when compared with the general population of Isabella, his native island. (Isabella is a mirror image of Trinidad which is Naipaul's own native land, though there are some elements of the narrative which are exclusive to the island of Jamaica.) But Jimmy has not come to terms with his twin historical and aboriginal heritage. This twin heritage, in fact, does not merge in any smooth way, but grate and jar upon one another. Jimmy is not fortunate enough to share Walcott's cure achieved in *Omeros*. Jimmy desperately wants the Englishwoman, Jane, to recognize his distinction from blacks, the very blacks he has dedicated his life to helping. In his diary—in the characteristically ungrammatical and grandiose style of the stereotypic mulatto—he projects this fantasy of distinction, truly the fracturing of his soul, as the musing of Jane:

> *I wonder how a man of those attainments can waste his life in a place like that with all those good-for-nothing natives for whom to speak in all candor I cannot have too high an opinion . . .*
>
> *You wouldn't believe that he can be so different from them. They live in poky little shacks on the highway and up the hills, any old piece of board and pitch-oil tin would do for them, you should see those shacks and then it will occasion no surprise that I have no great regard for these natives. But Jimmy's house is something else . . . He's obviously a man of considerable refinement rare for these days.*[9]

Jimmy's identity is pathological. Despite his overwhelming Eurasian heritage he is cast onto that heritage—African—to which he has the least claim, and which has the least resources for absorbing and accommodating his many incongruities. What Naipaul ends up showing with the character of Jimmy is the half-breed's innately incongruous, even hypocritical assumption of a 'black' identity. As many another half-breed, Jimmy turns away in anger from the vast resources of his historical heritage. Lacking the courage to claim this heritage, he falls upon the one which has neither the power to reject him or fulfill him. He assumes the usual role of mulattoes towards blacks—custodians, defenders, saviors, —made possible by their *non*-African heritage. Unwittingly, he has taken up Kipling's "white man's burden." But this characteristic role of the mulatto is simply a displacement of personal predicament. The mulatto carries within himself the contrary metaphoric worlds of Africa and Europe. But for Jimmy and many others, the European lineage is the stronger, the more resourceful and is the one which carries the degraded African heritage as burden, though this is never acknowledged. In his diary Jimmy 'safely' vents this repression by having it come from (his fantasy of) Jane:

They say he was born in the back room of a Chinese grocery, a half black nobody, just a Chinaman's lucky shot on a dark night, that's a good laugh, but I can see he is a man of good blood, only someone of my class can see that, to me he is like a prince helping these poor and indigent black people, they're so shiftless no one will help them, least of all their own.[10]

To anyone honest enough with himself, Jimmy Ahmed's agony in *Guerrillas* is as profound as Walcott's persona in *Omeros*. That Jimmy's agony is resolved negatively, or not resolved, is beside the point. What is important is the giving of expression to such deep feeling, such pathos.

But where Jimmy Ahmed failed, Naipaul the writer has triumphed. What he has stated elsewhere (in "A Plea for Rationality") as pertaining to his father, I believe also pertains to Naipaul himself: that one can have his sense of self—which is necessarily congenital and parochial—so transformed by one's experiences as to bode either good or ill, either opening up oneself to a world of great possibilities or causing one to stifle all future growth. These two avenues are found in both *Guerrillas* and *A Bend in the River*. Some characters accept the larger world while others try to hold it back to their detriment.

Naipaul gives the negative response as the reason why his father never developed as a writer, but attributes his own continued development as a writer to a positive self-transformation. It is quite clear that Naipaul's earliest sensibility was incompatible with the stereotypic West Indian identity. He certainly was never alone in this. However, because of particular social circumstances, Naipaul may not have been able to defend this sensibility or justify it to himself. As a writer he would cloak his deep estrangement in humor. True expression for him would come only when he decided to take himself and his alienation seriously. This was not as easy as it might seem, for as he himself would admit, it required a rejection of those premises upon which his view of the world was based.[11]

One can see the stark difference between Naipaul's early writings and those dating from the mid-nineteen seventies. In these later works one can clearly see that Naipaul's frame of reference is a universal one, in the true meaning of the word. This universal vision is no doubt the fruition of Naipaul's lifelong sensibility of renunciation which all his writings attest to. Though this new vision has been criticized as being the 'colonizer's,' one realizes that though this is basically true, Naipaul is so acclaimed by the Western world because he has rediscovered a vision which has somewhat dimmed within Western civilization and which has been the guiding light of all civilizations, not only the West.

Though Naipaul's vision is often seen as callous and even cruel, it is my belief that such a vision could only have been acquired with the greatest of moral honesty. The writer Naipaul did not sell his soul to the devil for success in his craft. It seems to me that Naipaul would have known he was assured the status as a world-class writer, a great writer, even without his transforming vision. However, this vision places him head and shoulders above the maudlin great who give expression to their ethnic milieu. Naipaul embodies the spark, the soul, of civilization and History.[12]

The callousness and cruelty that Naipaul is often accused of (especially in regard to these two books) could just as pointedly be applied to the renouncers of ancient India for their abandonment of their family and caste identities. Naipaul's personas have rejected not only the more insular Brahman-caste and Indian identities but also the larger West Indian (and by implication black) identity. But no one can deny the underlying moral tenacity of the renouncers' discipline. How could this discipline be ethical in the world of ancient India, but unethical in the context of the modern Caribbean?

Jimmy Ahmed in *Guerrillas* embodies the ideology of bondage, of imprisonment and pain, a victim's ideology. For Jimmy believes in his heart that he is a victim. He cannot stand back from his pain and its displacement unto others. He does not understand that liberating vision of Salim, the protagonist/narrator of *A Bend in the River:* "The world is what it is. Men who are nothing, who allow themselves to become nothing, have no place in it."[13]

In *A Bend in the River,* Salim's vision is a fully developed renouncer's vision. It is this vision which he turned mercilessly upon his own Indian community, his own family's particular Islamic tradition, and the surrounding black population of Africa. This novel is Naipaul's masterpiece simply because it is the first consummate expression of that "self-knowledge" which he himself had acquired. The main character, Salim, is the first of Naipaul's protagonists to forcefully take control of his life.

When Salim pitilessly peels away the ennobling metaphorical bandages of the European woman, Yvette, whom he becomes romantically involved with, he is doing no more than the renouncers of ancient India who cultivated a healthy repugnance for the human body. But Salim's 'repugnance' includes the society itself that he was born into. This is the Third World as depicted by Naipaul. It is also the Buddha's vision of the human condition. And Salim, without any apologies, seized his salvation:

And the decision I came to then was this. I had to break away. I couldn't protect anyone; no one could protect me. We couldn't protect ourselves; we could only in various ways hide from the truth. I had to break away from our family compound and our community. To stay with my community, to pretend that I had simply to travel along with them, was to be taken with them to destruction. I could be master of my fate only if I stood alone.[14]

The experience from which Salim has developed his renouncer's vision is that of the Indian communities in East Africa, and by extension, from those Indian communities in the Caribbean through the writer himself, Naipaul, who hails from such a community on the island of Trinidad. Here, as in East Africa, the Indian communities were besieged by the newly acquired notions of nationalism among the surrounding African populations. Once the pawn of the British in the fever of their own empire building—the Indians were brought to these black colonies as indentured labor—they were now abandoned by the British to "another tide of history," the African's own awakening to history. It is this buffeting about by other men's histories that Salim is lamenting.

An earlier "tide of history" which had wreaked havoc with a more original India was, of course, Islam. And it is Islam which comes in for Salim's most unequivocal rejection. Islam is Salim's family heritage, and it is the sacred in the form of Islam that he turns his back upon. The Arabs, themselves, have their ennobling metaphorical bandages mercilessly stripped by Salim, especially those Arabs who had made London their home. And earlier, Salim sees the plight of the Arabs in East Africa—the loss of their historical and civilized heritage—as an unspeakable tragedy. Salim (and Naipaul) is doing a thorough housecleaning. Not even Hinduism is spared. Indar, in his brief search for an ancestral Indian identity when he goes on an interview to the Indian embassy in hopes of becoming an Indian diplomat, ends up discovering a deep and irreconcilable alienation from classical Hinduism. Indar, at this point, looks upon classical Indian culture from the vantage point of an already alienated heritage—Islam—whose center was outside of India.

It is Indian society that Naipaul indicts so harshly. This book is Naipaul's masterpiece because it addresses something which must be at the heart of his concerns: the fate of those Indian communities estranged from their ancestral homeland on the subcontinent. Naipaul's literary persona does not seek an ancestral identity anymore than Walcott's persona seeks an African identity. Salim's relationship to India is rather like Walcott's poetic persona's relationship to Africa. Both have equal affiliations outside these identities. Salim is Muslim, a religion and tradition invading India from Arabia. And the heritage of Walcott's persona is largely

European. For both, in respect to ancestral homes, "There could be no going back; there was nothing to go back to. We had become what the world outside had made us; we had to live in the world as it existed."[15] But Naipaul's estrangement goes even further, or one might say, cleaves even closer to the present. The Indian communities of East Africa and the West Indies are looked upon as alien, as squatters even. They have even been expelled from Uganda.

No doubt it is this reality that has forced upon Salim his antipoetic vision. In *A Bend in the River,* when the family servant boy, Ali, comes to live with him, the African women see him as an exotic, and give him a new name which reflects his mixed-race heritage, *Métis,* a French word. Salim refuses to share the natives' admiration of Ali, refuses to acknowledge a poetic and classical French image of the boy, and to him the boy is Metty, a connotation which strips the word *métis* of any classical or exotic associations. This is a trademark technique of Naipaul. His preferred designation for New World Africans is the word "Negro," a word commensurate with their slavery, and a word detested by many. But Naipaul deliberately uses such a word to create distance, even alienation. Such a technique keeps his subjects at a distance, clothes Naipaul in surgical garb, as it were, and allows him, scalpel in hand, to dissect his subjects' (and his own) experiences. He never allows his subjects to sit with him, as it were, refusing to grant them that poetic vision and metaphoric world which they crave. And so he does not use the classical and more euphemistic 'African' when referring to the former slaves of the New World, avoiding the romance of the ancient Latin world. He prefers to use the word which retains closer association with that defining social experience, slavery, which is shared by Africans in the New World. But Salim's vision is also a quantum vision, a vision of fragmentation, not transcendence. To Salim there was no transcending unity in precolonial Africa. Salim does not share the flippant modern view that similar color of skin makes for an automatic brotherhood. Salim sees precolonial African identity as cultural, tribal. Different tribes never claimed any transcending unity. It is only with the coming of the Europeans, and truly only in an American context, that a transcendent African identity has been sought. (This was the legacy of Marcus Garvey.) But then, an identity only in reaction.

★

With Walcott and Naipaul the West Indian experience has achieved historical expression, that is, acquired form in a medium commensurate with civilization. These two writers have produced our great corpus of writing, our bible. In *Omeros,* Walcott constructs the most sublime metaphorical edifice upon the West Indian cultural experience. Naipaul, in *Guerrillas,* deconstructs the same West Indian experience to its frightening core where nothing holds it together, nothing redeems it. Both reveal the West Indian soul. Those who despise Naipaul must believe they can achieve a healthy synthesis of their racial and colonial legacy of alienation by denial and evasion. They must think that if one does not acknowledge ugliness and impotence, it will cease to exist. But just as Walcott, in *Omeros,* resolves his mulatto consciousness into its two antithetical components, the European sensibility of Plunkett and the African sensibility of Achille, so too the larger West Indian experience is resolved into the Christian missionary's compassion and the dispassionate vision of the Indian renouncer. This latter alienating vision, I dare say, is as much the heritage of the West Indies as Walcott's more accommodating stance. Naipaul's pitiless vision is just what the early Indian Buddhists sought to achieve when they followed the Buddha into the homeless life, and just as moral.

Naipaul's historical vision is in very sharp contrast to the poetic vision of Walcott. While Walcott's poetic persona agonizes over an inability to defend the poor and unfortunate, Naipaul's Salim takes recourse in the unflinching vision that men can look only to their own actions for salvation. Though one should be aware that Walcott's persona agonizes over an ideology of hate which he cannot bring himself to believe in. Walcott's poetic persona is not totally alienated from the historical world. But the persona's acceptance of this greater historical reality is always mitigated by its sympathies for the aboriginal current of its twin heritage.

Naipaul's personas, on the other hand, are never hesitant in seeing the modern industrial world as the reference for all reality. In *A Bend in the River* Indar admits (and Salim concurs) that, "For someone like me there was only one civilization and one place— London, or a place like it. Every other kind of life was make-believe."[16] One might say that the cynicism in Walcott's poetic persona towards historical society is because of its joint aboriginal heritage. But one is led to think that Naipaul, as an East Indian, is also heir to the Dravidian heritage of southern India, but which he can ridicule as Walcott would never dream of ridiculing things African. And in *The Mimic Men,* the narrator/protagonist leaves no doubt about which ancestry he claims. This is the Aryan heritage of India which early European tribes brought with them to the lands of the Indus and Ganges river more than three millennia ago. Walcott's poetic persona claims a partial African bloodline. Salim's and Naipaul's African influence is due to cultural proximity, a proximity, though, one suspects, which often seems like a blood-link, from which either cannot get too far.

Salim's vision is fundamentally utilitarian, even unforgiving in its pragmatic stance. It is one which experience has taught him. Walcott's poetic vision, on the other hand, is conjuring, celebratory, invoking, and seeks to *bring* a vision to the world, not to sift one from life's experiences. Walcott's persona debates and agonizes over its very real alienation from a superimposed West Indian identity. Naipaul's personas, on the other hand, are confident, even cocky in their own alienation from this same identity.

The poetic vision is Einstein's classical vision in the face of the new quantum physics which he, himself, had helped initiate. Confronted with Neils Bohr's new vision, Einstein declares: "Neils, God does not play dice with the world." The revolutionary Einstein was played out. Salim, like the quantum physicist Neils Bohr, inhabits a new world of the uncertain, unhampered by the classical forms of the old. Salim's world, like Neils Bohr's, is a world of pragmatism, a world with no transcendent vision, no ideal forms, truly a quantum realm, a realm that accepts experience without preconceived notions.

The metaphoric vision of Walcott's poetic persona does not capture the entire world of black people's reality. Take away the metaphors and you are left with the harsh light of the Naipaulian vision. Are either of these two visions superior? Or are they simply the different sides of the same coin? Walcott's vision is the more accommodating; but Naipaul's is not accused of falsehood, rather of exposing an existing vulnerability and pain, of exposing to the ridicule of the world a real shame, degradation and impotence. Is there no redeeming value in glaring truth? Is the method of seeing through the eyes of hopelessly alienated metaphors so unquestionably superior to an unadorned vision? Is the clothing in another man's ill-fitting robes so unquestionably superior to ones own nakedness? Is beauty so inherently superior to truth? Or is it, as another poet has said, one and the same: "Beauty is truth, truth beauty,—that is all/ Ye know on earth, and all ye need to know."?[17] To me there is nothing more sublimely beautiful than Walcott, nothing more glaringly truthful than Naipaul.

These two visions—the poetic and the historical—are reflected in the central question of the European enslavement of Africans. Walcott's treatment of this subject starts with the conventional black position, which depicts the culpability of European civilization. But the poet's persona has always extended a hand of forgiveness as in "Ruins of a Great House" (from *In a Green Night,* 1962). This amnesty, though, has become somewhat complicated in the persona's relationship to the United States, a nation which has historically been very hostile to the mulatto's assertion, as does the poet's persona, of a European heritage.

Naipaul's treatment couldn't be further apart. In *A Bend in the River* Salim notes the inherent fragmentation of native African society. In his portrayals of sub-Saharan African characters—

whether in Africa or in the New World—Naipaul views these as products of aboriginal culture and society confronting for the first time the technological trappings of civilization. To Naipaul's personas, it is always the unsubstantial nature of precolonial African society which is most responsible for the plight of Africans today. These societies were not viable and could not protect its citizens or even without slavery or colonialism prepare them for accommodation to technological civilization.

In accusing Naipaul of an exile's posturing, his detractors are guilty of a euphemism. Can they really believe that Naipaul's vision is simply a result of his exile status? that such a vision could only come from the 'colonizer's' home turf? They are guilty of much more than a euphemism. They are guilty of cowardly evasion in their refusal to see such a vision as essentially West Indian. Those who hold it to be so are those who see the West Indies as singularly African, who make no room for the East Indians, the Chinese, the Portuguese, and other European populations and influences, unaware that it was Europe who created the West Indies and even their own black identity. Do they think for one second that the East Indian has abandoned his own heritage and thrown in his lot with the African? The refusal to see Naipaul's vision as having its roots and stronghold in a home-based East Indian community may be nothing more than the oversimplification of black consciousness which sees everything non-African as 'white' or European, an unsophistication whose unchanging conceptual poles are a black/white racial dialectic. It may also stem from an insecurity which is afraid of acknowledging such a powerful and unflinching vision in a fellow competitor.

Naipaul's more alienated stance proceeds from the antagonism that exists between the Indian and black populations in Trinidad and Guyana, in particular, but which is ubiquitous wherever East Indians and blacks live in close proximity. An antagonism which Walcott glosses over, but which is as strident as any that peoples of different heritage may experience. Naipaul's narrative posture is not in reality an exile's posture as it is the vision of the core of a community which upholds a different and historical tradition, an ancient civilized sensibility (however creolized) which the surrounding black population does not equal, except in its pretensions to a European tradition.

Would those who defend a black identity refuse Naipaul the right to defend his own cultural heritage? Should Indians defer to black identity in a suicidal miscegenation? How utterly foolish of anyone to think that blacks and Indians are the same because they are Third World peoples together? Or that they live in harmony? *That* is the clumsy colonizer's alienated vision. It would only be the insular Indian heritage that would be destroyed. Black identity, having no consummate forms, being only the refuse of every other stable form, would swallow it without so much as blinking. And yet, the right by which such defenders claim the right to their own parochial identity, they deny to the Indian communities. It is the inferiority inherent in black identity, its intrinsic dependency, which makes it crave the condescension of every other identity.

That Naipaul's ancestors are East Indians does not make him any less a West Indian than Walcott. Both plumb a common West Indian experience for meaning. In both, the African influence in the Caribbean is merely background, though vitally essential background. Because of this surrounding back- and foreground of African influence Naipaul is as much a cultural mulatto as Walcott. His privileged and insulated East Indian upbringing parallels Walcott's own privileged childhood, whose European ancestry as much alienated and shielded him from the harsh realities and deprivations of the majority black population. Such an upbringing also failed to instill in Walcott a fundamental 'black' identity.

Both Naipaul's and Walcott's personas had their formative identities outside of the black experience. Naipaul was brought up as an orthodox Hindu, a Brahman. Walcott's poetic persona's formative identity came out of a European sensibility. Both employ these early identities in their approach to the black experience. Walcott's poetic persona is the quintessential European missionary's. The persona believes in a defining core identity. Thus in

Omeros (p. 218) the persona is afraid (but drawn to the idea, nonetheless) of losing this core identity or soul, which in its case at least is rather tenuous.

Naipaul, the world renouncer, has his personas turn away from this West Indian and black experience, even disdain it. What this renunciation releases them from is nothing more than racial (or blood-) identity, the *soul* of the modern world. In *The Mimic Men* Singh contemplates his "extinction":

I belonged to a small community which in this part of the world was doomed. We were an intermediate race . . . capable of disappearing in two generations into any of the three races of men, with perhaps only a shape of eye, or flexibility of slender wrist to speak of our intrusion . . . But what release to be the last of one's line![18]

The antidote to a blood-identity—Naipaul's "self-knowledge"—is nothing short of the most refined historical awareness. In "A Plea for Rationality" Naipaul advocates a vision of the ancestral past like that which came to Europe with the Renaissance—that is, a scholarly and unsentimental perspective. Indeed, it was only with the Renaissance that people accepted the reality of their times and the circumstances that determined their lives. Before then, people literally *lived* in the past. The mythic world-view of the Middle Ages enshrined the past, and in so doing diminished the lives of everyone. Not until men believed that their lives worked with the same reality as any other age that Europe could truly know itself. Thus Naipaul defines for us the renouncer's goal. By his own admission he himself had rejected the very idea of a soul (the **atman** in Hinduism), caste (Brahman), and race. Naipaul's renunciation, by excluding the atman and caste, took on aspects of the Buddha's own renunciation.

For the true exile, Walcott's poetic persona is the necessary past, Naipaul the present. Walcott's poetic persona exists in memory and recollection, Naipaul in the most glaring immediacy and actuality. Naipaul's vision is of total detachment, even alienation. His personas have climbed out of the pain inherent in the West Indian cultural milieu, and there is no road leading back to it. Walcott's vision of a particular West Indian anguish is the conventional one: he looks through a telescope at the West Indian cultural experience and everything is amplified tenfold, surrounding and inescapable. Naipaul does the unconventional and seemingly perverse: he turns Walcott's telescope around and looks through the far end, making Walcott's eyepiece his own objective lens. The West Indian experience observed in this way is just as clear as Walcott's, but now it is flung at an incredible distance, allowing the observer the greatest of objectivity, that cold vision which looks on itself indifferently and allows no Achilles' heel, no ethnic and parochial stance.

While the historical consciousness of Walcott's poetic persona is unstable—it retreats to aboriginal refuge when there is stress or conflict—that of Naipaul's personas is perfectly secure. Naipaul's personas, for example Salim, have thrown in their lot with civilization for better or worse. This does not make them in any way less West Indian than Walcott's. Both authors stand behind their cultural heritage equally, and both positions may be seen to express each author's respective heritage. Naipaul's unwavering commitment to a historical awareness may be seen to reflect his Indian heritage's age-old marriage with civilization. Walcott's heritage being both European and African is only partially committed to the historical awareness of his Aryan ancestors, his other commitment being to the preliterate societies from which the slaves carried to the New World were taken.

One should beware of stereotyping Naipaul, thinking that, as an East Indian, his identity is not compromised or even seriously undermined by the West Indian experience. As equally true for Naipaul as Walcott, the 'classics' of Old World literature have proved inadequate, and so both have endeavored to rewrite these to fit a new world. Naipaul's personas are the ones who have found it necessary to renounce caste, race, and nationality. But even though one cannot categorize Walcott's poetic persona as being defined by these, yet the persona still defends such categories on behalf of others.

Both Walcott and Naipaul have dealt severe blows to Marcus Garvey's ethnocentric world. But Walcott's poetic persona has remained significantly mired in this world. On the other hand, Naipaul's blow to this world has been fatal. Walcott's colonial vision is a tremendous advancement over Garvey's ethnocentric vision. But Naipaul's historical vision has broken that final bond which still holds Walcott's poetic persona. Naipaul's vision was always latent in the West Indian experience, and is indeed its supreme triumph. It is only in this purest of historical visions that Walcott's poetic persona can find its true manhood.

Walcott is our Homer. But like the Greek Homer whose poetic vision was revised by the later and more penetrating historical inquiry of Herodotus and others, so Walcott's vision finds its greatest refinement in the historical vision of Naipaul. The amazing thing is that they are both contemporaries, so Naipaul is not seen as *re*vising Walcott, but only as contradicting. Naipaul is our Herodotus. Or, one might say, our Plunkett (in *Omeros*) to Walcott's Achille. However inadequate one might see Plunkett's historical research into St. Lucia's past, however slanted, it is based on much more valid criteria than his counterpart's. Achille's invocation of his African past is dreamlike. It is through a trance—with his conscious perception suspended—that he conjures up his past. Though I would be the last to deny the place of this method.

Naipaul's vision does not debase Walcott. Rather it enables Walcott's sense of himself. Naipaul's vision defends Walcott's insistence on his mulatto sensibility. Blacks, in reaction, have inherited the same indiscriminate vision that Europeans have had of West Indians, and would deny Walcott his ethnic distinction. When western critics look at Walcott's poetry, the mere presence of African forms (incidental or not) makes it, according to their gross definition, a 'black' poetry. They do not realize that what draws them to it is its European sensibility, its historical filter. This is Walcott's unwavering reference. The truth is, also, that Walcott is generally rejected in the West Indies for being *too* European. Of course, one may argue that the possession and literary use of a European sensibility does not thereby make one European or white. But such an argument would also apply to an Afrikaner writer of Boer extraction who imbibes into his European sensibility the world of the African Zulus and Xhosas around him. One would instantly object that that could in no way change his European identity: so that the basis of identity would always be racial. In Walcott's case, the epithet 'black' would be grossly inaccurate and would do great injustice to an African identity which would seek as pure a form as its European counterpart. And, in any case, Walcott's blood heritage is European. The historical view of racial identity, this soul of the modern world, always breaks this up into its constituent parts. Doing so, one sees there is ultimately no atom of racial identity, no matter how far back in time one's racial type originated. The historical view rejects such gross and transcendent terms as 'black' or 'African.' Identity is not a whole but is always made up of constituent parts. The European, though, in his self-interest reserves the right of distinction and denies it to others. This is what Naipaul observes in the case of Belize (in "A Plea for Rationality"), but it is equally true of any West Indian island.

Neither is Walcott's poetic persona satisfied with a black identity for itself. In poem LI of *Midsummer* (1984) the persona seeks to place itself within its European heritage by seeing itself as a "raceless critic." But laments the reality that some will always seek to make it place its identity upon its partial African bloodline. In the poem's menagerie the reptilian member adamantly inscribes the persona within the genre of "Black Poets."

At the same time, to the persona (speaking on behalf of others) a purified historical sensibility is a betrayal to the islands' true identity. It is right in one sense. Naipaul's alleged betrayal is towards black identity, an identity which is intrinsically determined by an aboriginal sensibility. It is certainly understandable that the first transcendence of this sensibility would be painful. It is not Naipaul who has to accommodate to West Indians. It is West Indians who have to accommodate to Naipaul. What Naipaul discards (or betrays, if you will) is the identity necessarily determined and produced by this primitive sensibility. To come to terms with Naipaul's vision, West Indians would have to forge a new identity within a historical sensibility. To reject Naipaul as non-West Indian is to reject an indigenous historical vision. To reject Naipaul is to decide that the West Indian experience cannot accommodate a historical sensibility.

★

Naipaul's renunciation is a noble one. But while I have implied that it is valid in the case of *negro* blood, it is a renunciation which Naipaul has always seen as the prerogative of his own ethnic heritage. In *The Middle Passage* (1962) Naipaul sees his closest ally (as an East Indian in the West Indies) in the Portuguese. But sees the mulattoes—though with an infinitely stronger resonance of the European in their make up than Naipaul—as invariably identified by *negro* blood. The same distinction which Naipaul craved for himself and for which he yearned to leave Trinidad, and eventually did, this same distinction he denied to others. Naipaul, the 'exotic Asian,' brushes aside the mulattoes' much more recent Caucasian inheritance and claims exclusively for himself a European affinity.

This fabulous belief in an indestructible identity or soul *(atman),* which Naipaul attributes to *negro* blood, is the central tenet of his Brahman heritage. And the color discrimination which he so keenly observes among the mulattoes is a corner stone of his own Indian culture, but solidified after three or more millennia into castes and blood classes; distinctions, though after so many centuries of miscegenation, which remain as much of an obsession among Indians as among mulattoes. So Naipaul certainly does not stand on firm ground in his high-minded treatment of West Indian society: all of the forms he ridicules he would have known intimately in his own ethnic background, just in a more settled or conventional mode.

Naipaul is himself a more ancient 'mulatto,' a product of the early Aryan migrations into Dravidian India. And in his Brahman heritage one does not have to look far to find forms that are reflective not of the European and mulatto elites of the West Indies, but rather of the blacks whom he so often ridicules: a depressed economic state and landless status (the Brahmans depended on charity from the ruling classes), the prescribing of blood-based salvation for society at large, the indulgence in self-righteous suffering, the guardianship of a world of ritual and sacrifice, and even the fashion of unkempt hair (practiced among blacks by the Rastafarians). These were the hallmarks of the Brahmans and reveal the true nature of their identity. Like it often seems the blacks are in modern society, the Brahmans were a sanctimonious priesthood which was placated by the ruling Kshatriya and merchant classes. But the Brahmans had a trump card against these other classes of ancient India. This was their claim to Aryan racial purity. And just as they had degraded the noble tradition of renunciation to a racial dogma, so Naipaul invokes this dogma in his early works to look with disdain on everyone with non-European blood, and even lower caste Indians. But this was an irrational and untenable position (which to Naipaul's credit he would see through), just as it was with the Brahmans of twenty-five hundred years ago. Then, it would take a 'mulatto,' the Buddha (who as a Kshatriya yet possessed the blood of the conquered and enslaved Dravidians or Sudras) to undermine this hypocritical stance of the Brahmans. For though they were reluctant to admit it, the Aryan heritage of the Brahmans had become as diluted as that of the Kshatriyas. It is in the Buddha's criticism of Brahmanism that we find all of the tools needed to resolve the West Indian dilemma, to find an escape from the sanctimonious claims of blacks and the prescriptions for the blood-based salvation of society by the various ethnic camps, and even from Naipaul's early pretensions to a racial aloofness.

II
The Dharma of History

The dharma of the Brahmans, the Buddha and the Mahayana

The Buddha was an inseparable part of the sixth-century B.C.E. Indian society that he was born into. In a very important way he was a second-class citizen of this society composed of four classes or estates. The Kshatriyas were warriors, the traditional military arm of the society. There was also a hereditary priesthood, the Brahmans. The two subordinate estates were the farmers and merchants (Vaisyas), and the servants (Sudras). The ranking of these estates was twofold: in addition to our own modern criterion of material wealth, there was the equally important moral gradation of society. This dual system was not redundant. Though the Buddha belonged to the ruling or warrior estate, all prestige in ethics and knowledge was the prerogative of the Brahmans. It was the moral criterion, which placed the Brahmans at the top of the scale, that the Buddha would challenge.

In addition, and very significantly, each estate was independent in its blood lineage. In other words, one's membership in one or another estate was determined by birthright. Though the relationship between the estates had a moral value (the Brahmans the highest, the Sudras the lowest) it was only through birth or 'rebirth' that this moral value, practiced in any one lifetime, came to fruition. One was a Brahman or priest by birth, a Kshatriya or warrior by birth, a husbandman by birth, a servant by birth. It was this contradiction, of assigning both a moral and a 'blood' value to the estates, that in the eyes of the Buddha made the Brahmans position so untenable.

The Dharma of History

The repository of moral value was the atman ('the soul' or 'Self'). Class or estate identity was determined by one's atman. It was the moral state of the atman which caused one to be born in one estate and not another. The inferior incarnations of the atman, however, could be ameliorated. Theoretically, one could purify the atman even in the present life, through Brahmanic meditation, and so identify it with **Brahma,** the supreme being. But this identification was the prerogative of the Brahmans and (theoretically) could only be presumed by the three higher estates. It was legally denied the outcastes or Sudras, the lowest estate. Historically, the Sudras were a conquered population, succumbing to the three higher classes who referred to themselves as 'Aryans' (aristocrats, nobles) and who had migrated into northern India from central Asia in the second millennium B.C.E.[1] This fact is not without significance, as we shall see. Even after the Buddha's time, one finds in the *Manusmrity,* an ancient lawbook of the Brahmans, the decree that molten lead be poured in the ears of low-castes who overhear the Brahmanic scriptures.

The Buddha came from the outskirts of this society, which was centered along the Ganges river, and to which he later emigrated. He was born among the Shakya people on the northern fringe of the Ganges basin in what is today the country of Nepal. He very likely grew up without the Brahman estate as a significant presence hovering over his own Shakya tribe which saw itself as members of the ruler estate of Kshatriyas. In other words, the young Buddha (from the clan of Gautama) would have grown up in every way as a true aristocrat. But as he grew older and became aware of the significance of the Brahmans he must have wondered as to this structuring of society. And so what he went in search of was the identity of the Brahmans, the purified atman. This wisdom, all of the *samanas*—those who adopted the homeless life—must have sought after: What makes someone a first-class citizen? In the India of their day it was the atman. But the Buddha could not find it. And after six years of searching, he was certain that he had achieved a preeminence of knowledge. There was no higher understanding to reach, he was convinced, and this level of understanding did not reveal the atman. The truth is, though, that if the Buddha were a Brahman by birth and working with the established religious language of the day, he could just as easily have given the name of atman to the character he realized and called Tathagata (thus traveled/in this way developed).

There is no doubt that the Brahmanic language of religion was originally a fairly consistent one, but had become stagnant when confronted with the new social realities of the Buddha's day. All knowledge is the same, and when the Buddha referred to previous buddhas, he was most certainly referring to the religious seekers in the past who had used the Brahmanic system. There is undoubtedly a 'self' to renounce and a 'self' to find. The Buddha had rejected the atman but found "Tathagata." But again, the Buddha was not a Brahman, and he had no stake in upholding a system which inherently denied him that preeminence of knowledge and achievement which he sought. As a Kshatriya or warrior-estate member, he could never achieve the highest moral status within the society. His virtue would have to wait for a new rebirth, according to Brahmanic lore, in order for him to achieve Brahman identity, and then he could never be sure. In truth and in fact, the 'purified' atman in the Buddha's day was only possessed by a Brahman and it could only be found by a Brahman. It was in reality their social identity, the foundation of the social structure. This was the level to which the atman had fallen, where once it had been the appellation for that same achievement which the Buddha designated as Tathagata.

Where the Brahmans saw a universal self (Brahma), the Buddha saw the void of nirvana. In Brahmanic practice (preserved in the *Upanishads,* oral texts which had existed for some generations before the birth of the Buddha) one realized the union of the atman and Brahma. The Buddha also identified himself with the universe, but minus the metaphysical principle of creation which the Brahmans saw Brahma as providing (S I 62). For the Buddha, outer reality was not configured, either as Brahma, or in any other way.

47

But even more surprising, the Buddha did not see the *inner* aspect of moral reality as possessing any configuration whatsoever. Where the Brahmans realized an atman (a purified soul or self-essence), the Buddha realized **anatta**—the unreality of a transmigrating self or soul. The Buddha rejected all notions of an eternal self-entity as existing behind ordinary consciousness. Yet he did define a contingent self which was certainly commensurate with the original meaning of the Brahmans' unconditioned self-entity or atman. This was variously named as the Tathagata (the Thus-traveled), the Buddha (the Awakened), the **Arhat** (the Worthy, the saint), the **Ariya** (the Noble or Pure Ones), whose nirvana revealed reality. The Buddha also accepted that the true Brahman was also a contingent character which was capable of achieving nirvana (the unconditioned). To be fair to the Brahmans, this was no doubt what they meant, though their idiom of expression was somewhat antiquated and imprecise. The Buddha himself thought that he was merely rediscovering what the Brahmans had lost. The truth of the matter is that it might not have been the Brahmans' idiom of expression that had changed, but rather the society itself. In any case, we see that the Buddha's dharma could be cast in the 'self' idiom of the Brahmans; and the Brahmans' doctrine, in all fairness, must be seen as referring to that same achievement of the Buddha.[2]

One thinks of the later Zen injunction that the meditator should slay any image of the Buddha that he encountered in his practice.[3] This is what the Buddha had done to the Brahman's atman, their very identity and the essence of all their virtue. It was also, in principle, what the Mahayana did in their Bodhisattva ideal, who always gave up the final attainment of nirvana to remain in **samsara** (the cycle of rebirths) to administer to the suffering. Nirvana—the great achievement of the Buddha—remained a selfish desire as far as the Mahayana were concerned, as long as there were suffering beings in the world. With the Mahayana, the Tathagata—the Thus-traveled (to Enlightenment), became the Bodhisattva—the Enlightenment (seeking) Being. The Mahayana also had to reintroduce the moral criterion of compassion in order to displace the dry meditation technique which had evolved among the early Theravada. (Though in later Mahayana tradition Zen would again resurrect the early Theravada overemphasis on the mere technique of meditation.) The Buddha, in rejecting the language of Brahmanism and writing a new one, in principle did no more than the Mahayana who modified the language of Theravada Buddhism. The Buddha's rejection of the contemporary language of religion was just much more original and far reaching.

There is hardly a doubt that the Bodhisattvas achieved the same awareness as the Theravada Arhats, despite their expressed rejection of 'nirvana.' The Mahayana's assertion that samsara and nirvana were the same was simply the Buddha's own assertion that "All created things are grief and pain—he who knows and sees this is at peace though in a world of pain; this is the way that leads to purity."[4] What the Buddha meant was that there was no euphoric, trancelike nirvana. The only true nirvana came when the disciple did not recoil from life's inherent frustrations, did not seek magical refuge from the full reality of phenomena. In short, nirvana was the recognition of the intrinsic frustrations of life. This was not stoicism, but true liberation. In the Buddha's dharma the disciple realized that frustration was only a function of atman. Dissolve the reference point of the atman and he dissolved constraint *(dukkha)*. But also he destroyed, in himself, the capacity to contribute to the social pain which the atman upheld.

This teaching was also the legitimate basis for the Mahayana concept of "emptiness" or Sunyata, which denied all absolute categories. This was an attempt to redefine the nirvana which they had rejected. But since in his very first discourse the Buddha had stated that "the five modes of clinging are constraining," nirvana (which was the extinction of constraint) could never be an absolute category. There was no room in the totality of the five modes *(khandha)* which comprised the individual—bodily form, expression, impression, configurations and entrancement—where its opposite (nirvana) could exist. It would, in fact, be a direct contradiction. The Mahayana insistence was a truism, for the very first Noble Truth invalidated nirvana as an absolute category. All things when conditioned were constraining, just as all things when not conditioned were seen to be without an atman and without constraint. The Buddha's "fathom-long carcass" comprised all things, both the "world" and the "transcendence" of the world.[5] Certainly, both samsara and the transcendence of samsara (nirvana) could and would exist over the same field of the five modes, for the transcendence of anything encompasses that thing, while at the same time is removed from all of it. Nirvana was the *outside* of the world and the *end* of samsara, neither of which could increase the world or samsara. It was the mathematical concept of zero— emptiness, voidness—which 'nirvana' designated, and which 'logic' it shares: the living cipher which made the Buddha's ciphering of his life so easy. Though there is indeed nothing in zero, it is certainly useful and very real when it is the 'zero' of constraint!

The contemporary Brahmans' atman had lost this quality of emptiness. Without their knowing it, the atman had acquired the very concrete manifestation of birthright. It was the social matrix, the social space—the right, the license, the social franchise (or not)—within which a person could say "I am," "You are," that alone defined that 'existence' which was relevant to the dharma. It was, in fact, the social existence of birthright. The only reality that was relevant to the dharma was that validation, that authentication, that sanctioning within the social matrix that was given to a birth. That other 'existence' of the physical was irrelevant. The Buddha did not invite any pertinent questions relative to the nonsocial realm, or offer any meaningful answers. His agnostic replies to Malunkyaputta's questions (M I no. 63) as to the dimensions of the physical universe and the soul limited the validity of the dharma to the social realm.

In contrast to the 'zero' of nirvana, the Brahmans' atman designated the materiality of the five modes. To uphold this degenerated atman, the Buddha realized, he would have to give up true learning, true development. He could never attain his goal of an eminence of understanding if he upheld the true essence of one's self as emanating from the preknowledge of birthright, of having its foundation in an inscrutability. The atman was self-contained. One could not add to it, or subtract from it, no matter what the Brahmans taught. As social reality they had achieved everything it could give. As a system of rational inquiry, though, it was dead. The Buddha could never have reached to an eminence of understanding within this system, with the atman, the ultimate understanding, defined the way it was.

The Buddha's moral rationality

But before the Buddha could justify the rejection of the atman he would subject himself to a very strenuous moral training. It was the moral that would be his most powerful weapon against the Brahmans. Contrary to popular belief, the Buddha's awakening did not take just one night. This view is based on the erroneous notion that it is yoga—merely a concentration of the mind—which is the basis of the Buddha's dharma or doctrine. What this view fails to recognize is that the Buddha was practicing a stringent moral conduct for six or more years before his awakening. This was the *moral rationality* which always ran parallel to his extreme asceticism. This moral rationality he would designate as the Eightfold Way of rational views, rational intention, rational speech, rational action, rational livelihood, rational application, rational recollection and rational study.

After six years of practicing a very extreme asceticism which had left him emaciated and weak, and one day having gone to the river Nairañjana to bathe where he swooned and nearly drowned but for the help of an overhanging tree-branch, the Buddha suddenly realized the uselessness of this practice. The all important role of choice or will in action (karma) became clear to him. It was at this point that he saw the causality in his life's actions, an understanding which broke the hold of rebirth. And so he accepted from Sujata—the daughter of a neighboring landowner—a bowl of milk rice, his first full meal in a very long time, and sat down to refine the concepts of this dynamic vision of personality.

The Buddha's enlightenment really occurred that evening when he understood the causality of self-mortification with its product of pain. But this understanding was not painful; it was entirely positive. And so he reached back to his childhood for the causality of that understanding (in contrast to the pain of self-mortification). And he recovered, as the prototype of this new understanding, a time when he had so worked on his mind to produce its great composure and rationality. These two currents, self-mortification (explicit or implicit) on the one hand, and rationality on the other—the positive and the negative, the "karma of pain" and the "karma of happiness"—had always operated side by side in the Buddha's life. On that fateful evening beside the river, the one that finally won out was understanding. When he sat down beneath the Bodhi tree it was merely to work out the conceptual form of this new understanding, a conceptualization which he had no doubt been mulling over in his mind for years. The crude forms of which he would have gotten from the Upanishadic lore of the Brahmans, for here there were many schemata of the dharma.

That night the Buddha would legitimize his long practice of a moral rationality in the doctrine of the Eightfold Way. This "path that leads to the end of constraint" was the last of the Four Noble Truths. The first Truth was that of "constraint." Though the entire life process was constraining, the core of this lay in the "clinging" to the five modes (of karma): body, expression, impression, configurations and entrancement. The second Truth identified the cause of this constraint as that compulsion (literally "thirst") in the service of rebirth: carnal compulsion, the compulsion favoring birthright, the compulsion rejecting birthright. The causal nature of compulsion lay in its impulsive forcefulness or urge which was contrary to the Buddha's own will, and which diverted him from his state of equilibrium. (It is the automatic, unthinking quality of impulse, intrinsic to compulsion, which so alienates it from the

52

rationality of the Eightfold Way, an absolute alienation which is not shared by the more common rendering as "craving," the motivation of which is identical with its focus of attention and so always known. And because craving can also be, and often is directed towards the positive and good, it can never be the causal agency of the negative constraint.) The third Truth stated that the end of constraint did in fact occur with the quiescence of this compulsion.

The Buddha would also define a chain of causation of constraint which consisted of twelve consecutive terms each of which conditioned the next. —THE PAST GENERATION: ignorance: configurations (of bodily form, expression, impression): entrancement: conceptualization: sentience: THE PRESENT GENERATION: communication: clinging: birthright: THE FUTURE GENERATION: constraint.[6] While the Eightfold Way was an elaboration of positive karma, this twelve-linked chain was an elaboration of negative karma which the Buddha had touched upon only briefly in the second Noble Truth of the cause of constraint. There this negative karma was given simply as compulsion. But in the chain of causation it was unfolded into as many as eleven distinct phases. By placing "ignorance" so early in the chain, however, the Buddha preserved the causality of constraint as *compulsion,* as that impulse—mental or physical—the origin of which was shrouded in an unknowing, the action done without consideration, without deliberation.

Though the doctrine of conditional origination is often equated with these twelve causal links of constraint it was not exclusive to this chain but pertained also to the Eightfold Way. Both the positive and the negative, the grossest evil and the purest virtue were conditioned by karma. The Buddha asserted (Sn 650–5) that the most positive character—Brahman—as well as the negative one of a thief were both governed by conditional origination. So conditional origination really had two aspects: one dealt with the causation (from a negative rebirth impulse) of constraint or suffering; the other dealt with the causation of the character, Brahman, with which one realized the unconditioned. But because even the highest reaches of the Eightfold Way were conditioned, one was compelled to give it up as a "raft" which had helped one to get to the far shore of a river (M I no. 22).

So it was at that moment when the rationality of the Eightfold Way—the positive in the positive—was fulfilled that the impulsive causality of the twelve-linked chain of causation—the negative in the negative—was extinguished. The Buddha's extreme asceticism did not culminate in his liberation. It was rather the Buddha's liberation which led to the unconditional rejection of the compulsion to self-mortification. His earlier rejection of desire and passion —when he left his family for the homeless life—marked the start of the intensive practice of a moral rationality. But in practicing self-mortification the Buddha was hoping to find salvation through pain. Such a method was inherently illogical, for it entailed finding the positive (salvation) through the negative (pain). But the Buddha had fortunately set in motion a process which would grow alongside the contradictory and barren method of extreme asceticism and eventually eclipse it. This was the practice of a moral rationality.

The Buddha would detail to a certain Saccaka (M I no. 36) his transition from extreme asceticism to the doctrine of the Middle Way. Though he had practiced self-mortification in the hopes that it would bear fruit in enlightenment, he would here relate that it was indeed the practice of a moral rationality, the abstention from "sensual pleasures," which had protected him from being destroyed by the pain of self-mortification: "But such painful feeling that arose in me did not invade my mind and remain."[7]

After six years of this debilitating practice he perceived that, "that conjoined with self-torture, [was] painful, ignoble, and useless."[8] He saw the course of all his life's actions: the positive in the positive, the negative in the negative. In recalling the positive causality in his life, he remembered a time in his childhood when he was taken by his father, the king, to the annual plowing festival of the Shakyas. Observing the inevitable destruction of creatures that the plowing of the soil entailed, he had retreated to the shade of a rose apple tree to ruminate on the nature of life. He resolved to return to a normal diet so that he might take up again this more rational practice of reflection (M I no. 36).

Six years earlier (and not long after he had left home for the homeless life) he had tried and rejected in turn the meditation practices of the Brahman teachers Arada Kalama and Udraka Ramaputra. Now again, as he sat down beneath the Bodhi tree he would be tempted by that earlier method and the pleasurable feelings which the relinquishing of mental functioning brings. Four times his concentration would be challenged by the allure of self-absorption, but each time he would prevail in his course of reflection: "But such pleasant feeling that arose in me did not invade my mind and remain."[9] It was only then, in this equanimity, that *rationality* was fully established in the Buddha, and he could attain to the four 'levels' of knowledge (corresponding to the four watches of the night) that constituted his enlightenment.

This four-staged progression of understanding obviously took the place of the four higher levels of self-absorption which the Buddha had practiced six years earlier under the two Brahman teachers. However, this new practice did not shun mental functioning as the attainments taught by these yogic teachers did. The Buddha's understanding that night was a complete rationality. This was the four Noble Truths and the understanding of conditional origination and the rebirth histories of himself and others. It may be the latter understanding that lends to the Buddha's enlightenment an aura of mysticism, but even this as we shall see was very rational. In the Discourse of Effacement (M I no. 8) the Buddha is very explicit that the practice of self-absorption (with its total of eight stages) was *not* the discipline that won nirvana:

It is possible here that . . . some bhikkhu enters upon and abides in the base of neither-perception-nor-non-perception [the last stage of self-absorption]. He might think thus: 'I am abiding in effacement.' But these attainments are not called 'effacement' in the Noble One's Discipline: these are called 'peaceful abidings' in the Noble One's Discipline.[10]

The truth is that the Buddha's realization of the evening (when he saw the uselessness of extreme asceticism) was of the same nature as the long night of meditation. When he sat down under the Bodhi tree it was simply to elaborate, and to put intellectual form to, his earlier realization. The product of the night was the concrete form of the Four Noble Truths and the chain of causation. This could certainly have been formulated in one night. And the Buddha having rejected trancelike (yoga) meditation, would have had no need for it for this purpose.

The Buddha never abandoned consciousness that night, or reason. What he rejected was the belief that reason applied exclusively to the mind organ, separate from the body's action, the moral. It was a complete rationality alone which won through to nirvana. The rationality of one's body, one's conduct, was inseparable from the mind's rationality. Emphasizing one over the other had given the Buddha the common misperception that they were intrinsically disunited. It was the body's reason which contained the fullest realization of the Buddha's character, and the fullest expression of the realm normally separated out as 'mind.' It was irrational impulse which formed mind. This was what the Buddha meant when he disparaged reason: it was the reason which could not embrace the body that was not viable—the mind's reason. The body's reason was morality, right conduct. This was the essence of the dharma. There was no practice without the body's reason, no nirvana without the body's truth. Speculations, rationalizations independent of the sphere of the body, engendered mind, created mind. And the body's truth, the body's reason— virtue—dispelled mind. That was why the monk in search of nirvana had first to look to the body's truth—honesty in conduct- —before anything else. And had to let this truth generate mental life. But the monk was always reminded that morality was first and always rationality, reason, honesty; it was not convention, custom, tradition or mere rule-keeping. The Buddha's basic guidelines for this bodily reason were kindness, gentleness, admiration, respect, politeness, the placing of value on every individual, and wanting for others the good things his disciples wanted for themselves. The true practice of dharma was a moral rationality:

Now, Cunda, here effacement should be practised by you:
   'Others will be cruel; we shall not be cruel . . .
   'Others will kill living beings; we shall abstain from killing living
       beings . . .
   'Others will take what is not given; we shall abstain from taking what
       is not given . . .
   'Others will be uncelibate; we shall be celibate . . .
   'Others will speak falsehood; we shall abstain from false speech here':
       effacement should be practised thus.[10]

To debase the body in self-mortification was to fail to realize that 'body' was just the woefully repressed original nature, and to exalt, instead, the shadows of mind. But enlightenment was only the coming to full consciousness of this repressed nature. That was why, when the Buddha realized the error of extreme asceticism, he immediately recalled a phase in his childhood which would be from then on the prototype for his adult behavior. It was this childhood mode which was the crux of his enlightenment. The Buddha had reached back to his original nature, preceding the entrance of mind and estate identity. It was this undefiled mode of experiencing which he would recommend to his monks.

But this original self was not the source of childlike or infantile behavior; it was not, in any way, an undeveloped mode of rationality or perception of reality. Rather, it consisted of those fundamental premises upon which the Buddha's life was based, his life's original, rational orientations, its strongest rational currents. The Buddha had reasserted his most basic individuality. And it was only natural that this individuality should be traced back to, and be perceived most clearly in childhood, before any conflicting and alienated valuation of himself had been ingested.

When the Buddha gave up the practice of extreme asceticism, he gave up the alienation of mind and body. The truth was, he gave up the vanity of mind which sought understanding independent of materiality. This was the meaning of "thought cannot see itself"; for the Buddha saw clearly that it was "impossible that anyone can explain . . . the growth, increase and development of consciousness, independent of bodily form, feeling, perception and mental formations."[11] This, sad to say, was the position of the Brahmans. Their fallen atman was a bundle of conflicts. Inseparable from estate identity, it was nevertheless spoken of as a 'spiritual' attainment. With his enlightenment the Buddha would see the Brahmans' atman for the totally negative phenomenon that it was.

The social context of the dharma

The atman of the Buddha's day, with its avowed inscrutable origins, was used to support a stagnant and morbidly hierarchical society. It served only to give an acceptance of one's status in an unchanging social structure. And so the Buddha in effect rejected his social identity, the secondary moral status of Kshatriya, which was the social manifestation of his atman.

Here one finds the social message of the Buddha. It was *identity* which structured society. So that rejecting this, the Buddha could include in his Order (Sangha) members of all the four estates. The forsaking of social identity was a prerequisite for membership in the Sangha, but it was also the final goal of the Buddha's discipline when one understood not through faith or belief, but in one's very own life, the fallacy of the notion of identity: " 'I am' is a vain thought; 'This am I' is a vain thought; 'I shall be' is a vain thought; 'I shall not be' is a vain thought. Vain thoughts are a sickness, an ulcer, a thorn."[12] It was the sickness of identity that the dharma cured.

The underlying conflict which prevented the Buddha from referring to his liberation (moksha) as the atman could only have been the conflict of estates. The Brahmans had monopolized the professional practice of ethical conduct. It must have really irked the Buddha that the Brahmans had a hegemony on philosophy and moral practice. At the same time, the Brahmans were encroaching upon the traditional Kshatriya monopoly of material wealth by accumulating the constant gifts of land and livestock that were made in exchange for their sacrificial duties. Coming from the opposite position, the Buddha was obviously at odds with his own prescribed role as a Kshatriya, what in the modern world would be a soldier-statesman. But the Buddha was not alone. The Kshatriyas were abandoning in droves their traditional role for that of the religious life, the longtime prerogative of the Brahmans. Needless to say, the Brahmans were resentful of this movement. In one exchange between the Buddha and a Brahman by the name of Esukari, the Buddha is accused of abusing his responsibility as a Kshatriya and of being no less than a thief by adopting the role of a religious seeker, a career choice reserved for Brahmans (M II 181).

The scriptures depict the young Buddha as a very sensitive child. As a young man the Buddha became obsessed with the fundamental questions of life. How great must have been his consternation to have this field of inquiry preempted by a class which excluded him. To someone of great self-worth this was unacceptable. It was only natural, then, that when the Buddha achieved his moksha or liberation he would refuse to attribute to it the quality which the Brahmans claimed preeminence in through birthright—the atman. The Buddha refused to deliver his supreme accomplishment into the hands of those who upheld an innate inferiority on his part. For the Brahmans certainly claimed that their present incarnation as Brahmans was morally superior to all other social classes. As a Kshatriya, the Buddha would have had to accept that, morally, simply by reason of birth, he was ill-equipped to achieve the supreme identification with the god Brahma. No doubt it was to combat this that the Buddha devised the doctrine of conditional origination. This doctrine made the Buddha's chances equal to the Brahmans in the quest for nirvana.

With conditional origination the Buddha denied that through birth one acquired a positive moral impulse: "Not by birth does one become a brahman; not by birth does one become a non-brahman. By action one becomes a brahman; by action one becomes a non-brahman."[13] Action or karma (that is, conduct) was seen as the only determinant of moral value. Identity or atman (from the supreme claim of Brahman to the lowest estate of Sudra) was the product only of the actions one performed in the present life. The doctrine of conditional origination denied that moral life was somehow automatic. One was not born with a consummate moral identity or atman, as the Brahmans claimed, but acquired one through conduct in one's life.

The meaning of rebirth and nirvana

Why was the Buddha not concerned with simply denying rebirth as he did the atman? To the Buddha one did not just deny rebirth, one *realized* its extinction: it was only after a long process of moral discipline that the Buddha declared the cessation of the mechanism of rebirth. The Western world's impatience with the Buddha's notion of rebirth stems from the fact that the Buddha, the consummate pragmatist, was not satisfied with a mere hasty denial. He applied the method of dharma—which made use of the moral character—to the question of rebirth. It was never simply denial which eradicated rebirth in the Buddha, but moral accomplishment.

The objection to rebirth from the standpoint of Western science is likewise applicable to the atman. Western science does not find support anywhere for an eternal entity, or a mechanism sustaining this entity. One might well ask, Where would this leave the dharma, since with science we have achieved the same result of the Buddha, namely, the nonexistence of an eternal soul and its underlying mechanism? The answer is: nowhere—if the atman is what we have said it is. We would then have no use for the dharma. One should realize, though, that unlike anything 'science' could detect, this atman was *moral* in character.

The Buddha saw *dukkha*—the very real constraint which

nirvana broke—as stemming from (the notion of) the atman. He referred to belief in an eternal self, or soul, as

mere views, a thicket of views, a puppet-show of views, a snare of views; and ensnared in the fetter of views, the ignorant worldling will not be freed from rebirth, from decay and from death, from sorrow, pain, grief and despair; he will not be freed, I say, from suffering.[14]

The atman, then, was 'real.' It produced results. We cannot deny, though, that while the atman was seen to exist as mere thought—illusion—rebirth was seen to exist independent of thought.

Was this emphasis begun by the Buddha? Very likely it was. The moral practice of the Buddha and the Brahmans differed in result with respect to the atman. The Brahmans realized the truth of the atman. The Buddha realized the atman's nonexistence. The Buddha was thus placed in the position of having to emphatically deny the existence of the atman. This guaranteed his emphasis on the doctrine of *anatta* (non-soul). This was not the case with rebirth. Moral practice obtained the extinction of rebirth for both the Brahmans and the Buddha. The nonexistence of rebirth was a built-in condition: it automatically ceased to exist with liberation (moksha). So the Buddha would have felt no pressure to emphatically deny rebirth as he did the atman, which latter (for the Brahmans) was thought to exist in liberation, which was in fact its natural condition. Feeling no special need to reject it, rebirth would then have acquired the status of greater reality than the atman.

Yet this could only be a superficial reason. For it is undeniable that the doctrine and practice of *anatta* played an all-important role in escaping the mechanism of rebirth. *Anatta* was intrinsic to the practice of dharma. This begs the question: why was the refutation of an illusion so central to the dharma? In fact, why was the process of *anatta* so crucial to escaping rebirth, which latter was the *designated negative reality?* The answer could only be that the atman was inextricably linked to rebirth, since refuting it freed one from rebirth. And since rebirth was reality (though negative) this aspect of the atman could not be the traditionally illusory or spiritual atman, the soul. The atman thus possessed a hidden or invisible dimension, but one which was very real indeed. It is this 'dark matter' of the atman which I will reveal.

For many (if not most) Western educated people the atman as 'soul' does not exist. Why, we even have a brand of philosophy—atheism—which enshrines the nonexistence of the soul. But no one claims that either of these positions is the way to nirvana. Obviously, either what we take to be the atman or soul today is not the same as in the Buddha's day, or the atman has a somewhat different manifestation which we fail to recognize. It is the former conclusion which seems most plausible. Some attempts have been made to finding the atman's modern expression. Most translations render it as Self or Ego. But this only serves to divest the atman of its traditional religious property of *transmigration,* since most people understand the self and ego as the material and psychological sheaths—in other words, as the five modes. It seems to me that these translators are in the same position as the Brahmans. Asked to distinguish this 'Self' from the Tathagata, who is without the Brahmans' atman and the translators' 'Self,' they would be at a loss; for the material and psychological sheaths (which most people understand the self and ego to be) cannot be extinguished by moral means as the dharma requires of the atman, and which the character of Tathagata achieves; they can only be physically destroyed. So it is doubtful whether these renderings have any religious value, that is, whether they are pertinent to the dharma. Since a basic self or ego remains even with the realization of nirvana, these designations might as well be used for that basic self. What these attempts fail to recognize is that there are two atmans—the positive atman of the Brahmans, and the negative atman of the Buddha.

A much more likely candidate for the modern context of the negative atman perceived by the Buddha is identity in all its variety, but especially ethnic and racial identities which are *intergenerational.* These blood-identities are more congruent to the full significance of the atman of the Buddha's day. They provide a static model of the self and the ability of this 'self' to survive across innumerable human generations. Neither the Self nor Ego, which translations render the atman as, is able to accomplish this. The expansive 'self' of racial identity is also commensurate to the blood-lineage or whole-estate status of the atman. The Self and Ego are much too individualistic to be equated with this mass identity of the atman.

A blood-identity is a static system of self. It is identical to the contemporary Brahmans' atman. Like the atman it creates itself out of the five modes of bodily form, expression, impression, configurations and entrancement; creates itself out of modes intrinsically impermanent, yet claims for itself intrinsic permanence. Like the atman it is conducive only to great pain and suffering by having its foundation in the irrationality of preknowledge. And like the atman, it is extinguished only with the perception of the dynamic mechanism of moral causality.

Only a blood-identity can fit that atman, in both its physical and moral aspects, that the Buddha renounced so passionately. 'Soul' does not possess the physical aspects of a blood-identity and the Buddha's atman. And 'Ego' and 'Self' do not possess the trans-generational dimension of the atman and blood-identity. The atman clearly was a blood-identity, and the reason that it was subject to rebirth was because a blood-identity was transgenerational.

The negative atman, by definition, existed across human genera-tions. It was only such an identity, one which underwent trans-migration, that one had to renounce (that one *could* renounce) to achieve nirvana. The dharma was only concerned with a *trans-generational self-entity or identity*. Today, this same identity, even the moderns declare, existed in their fathers' day, their grandfa-thers' day, their great-grandfathers' day, ad infinitum; and subject themselves to its continuance by projecting it into the future, ad infinitum. And those coming after them will also lay claim to it. Despite all their protestations to the contrary these moderns do believe in rebirth, after all!

Were the ancients superstitious in believing as they did? Was their belief in a transmigrating identity any stronger than ours?

Racial identity and the degenerate atman of the Buddha's day proceed from the same deep structure. Without being fully conscious of it in the way that we are today, they were yet dealing with the same thing. It makes perfect sense now why the Buddha, being himself so rational, could still insist on the truth of samsara, a transmigrating, transgenerational identity. There was a very real basis for the Buddha's belief; it was essentially a 'racial' (or blood-) identity that the atman had come to designate. Our own modern belief in a transgenerational identity certainly dwarfs that of the ancients.

It is the rejection of a blood-identity which is most in harmony with the quenching or extinction found in the Buddha's nirvana. The material and psychological self or ego which remains after the extinction in nirvana is achieved is not irrelevant or inconsequential. This basic self is the home of the moral rationality which achieves the extinction of the Gargantuan 'self' of blood-identity. The modern context for this positive self or ego, which the Brahmans insisted their atman designated, is nothing other than the ultimate individuality. What the ancient sages of the *Upanishads* sought to achieve were the farthest reaches of an individualism and self-assurance. This original atman—in its identification with the universal Brahma—was always the transcendence and antithesis of a blood-identity; it was always an ultimate *individualism* to which was attributed the greatest of integrity and morality.

Throughout the Brahmanic tradition there had always been two atmans: the atman of rebirth, encumbered with ill-virtue, mired in blood-identity, and the atman of moksha, the extricated atman, the freed atman. "That thou art" was the refrain of the *Upanishads,* and this "thou" (the atman, the "self") was taught to identify with the multifarious universe—Brahma—away from the claustrophobic identities of blood. But by the time of the Buddha, even the 'extricated' atman led only to another 'blood' group, the birthright Brahmans. The transcendent self of the universal Brahma—its unborn and unconditioned properties—the Buddha incorporated in his own nirvana, and upheld the validity of the character of the

Brahman which perceived this reality. It was the opposite identification of the self with lineage chauvinism, the traditional imprisonment of the atman, which the Buddha rejected, for in this new social reality the multifarious universe of Brahma was defined back to its antithesis of a blood-identity.

When the Buddha rejected the Brahmans' atman it was not an occult or even transcendent entity that he defined. The rejected atman consisted of real material qualities and discernable psychological phenomena—eye, ear, nose, tongue, views, concepts, emotions, etc. The atman was, in fact, estate and clan chauvinism, both of which were based on blood. The overwhelming constraint of this to the Buddha was obvious. In one telling passage it was likened to a dog "tied on a rope to a strong pike or pale":

Likewise, Bhikkus, the unschooled common person looks upon the body thus, 'This is my own,' 'I am this,' 'This is my identity,' . . . he looks upon expression . . . impression . . . configurations . . . entrancement thus, 'This is my own,' 'I am this,' 'This is my identity.' If he goes, he goes towards these five modes of clinging; if he stands still, he stands close to these five modes of clinging; if he sits down, he sits close to these five modes of clinging; if he lies down, he lies close to these five modes of clinging.[15]

It was this very attachment to the five modes which was the bane of the Buddha. He would make it, in fact, the first of his four Noble Truths, the truth of *dukkha* or constraint: "In essence, all of the five modes when clung to are constraining." It was really only within this clinging to body, expression, impression, configurations and entrancement that all the other constraints listed in the first Truth unfolded (of rebirth, old age, sickness, death, etc.).

It was the identification with the five modes that had grown the Buddha's malignant self. He would seek, at first, to remove its constraint through self-mortification. He would later reject this very 'physical' approach and define a purely 'moral' one. For self-mortification, the Buddha later explained (D III no. 25), was a sanctimonious practice and led only to vanity and hypocrisy. It was concerned only with outward appearances, and left untouched the heart or "pith" of things. In other words, it increased the very thing which it outwardly sought to destroy.

By abandoning his own practices of self-mortification, the Buddha rejected the notion that suffering was a basis or substitute for virtue. This was a much greater revelation than is normally thought, for it was only the Buddha's great compassion for the poor and unfortunate that alone could explain his six years of self-mortification. It was the identification with the suffering of others which this practice allowed which held the Buddha for so long. But this morbid empathy with the pain of others was not conducive to the Buddha's own heart or "pith," which remained constrained. The wider implication of his rejection of self-mortification was that no matter how much he himself or others may suffer, this did not of itself bestow virtue. It was the destruction of the toxic identity of the five modes—an identity which self-mortification reinforced—which would release the Buddha from his constraint. He placed the creation of this identity not on others but within oneself:

The venerable Radha said to the Exalted One: " 'a kind,' 'a kind,' one is assigned. Regarding what, Lord, is one assigned 'a kind?'"

"As a result of being conjoined and amalgamated by that desire, that attraction, that eagerness, that compulsion towards body . . . towards expression . . . towards impression . . . towards configurations . . . towards entrancement, accordingly one is assigned 'a kind.' "[16]

The Buddha's rejection of this malignant self was both uncompromising and sublime. In answering his disciple, Radha, who asked the above question, the Buddha drew an analogy between the mud-pies of little children's games and the identity created through the attachment to the five modes. And just as these little boys and girls would lose interest in their games and without any hesitation scatter to the winds what they had only a moment ago taken such pleasure in, so Radha was to treat the five modes:

Even so, Radha, you should scatter body, destroy it, tear it down, stop pampering it, you should practice so as to overcome the compulsion towards it. You should scatter expression . . . impression . . . configurations . . . entrancement, destroy it, tear it down, stop pampering it, you should practice so as to overcome the compulsion towards it.

Truly, Radha, is nirvana the voiding of compulsion.[16]

Another striking imagery used by the Buddha was that of painting. In the *Samyutta Nikaya* (III 152) the Buddha likens the unwise person's ascription of reality to the five modes, to the painter's reproduction of the human form. It was through the arresting mechanism of *identity* that the highly stylized renderings of the five modes were produced, rather as an artist captures an image of the real world.

In the Buddha's case, the two significant 'paintings' or 'arrested images' of these five modes were his blood-identities of estate and clan—Kshatriya and Gautama. These were always seen as a lesser reality than the unstyled modes. Still, never a pleasant or aesthetic image for the Buddha, but a truly horrific one. For what the Buddha annihilated with his nirvana were "the bodily form, the expression, the impression, the configurations and the entrancement" of this fabrication or counterfeited reality, this 'ghost.'

The more pervasive analogy used by the Buddha, of course, was of identity as a fire drawing on the five modes for fuel. Thus rebirth came to be seen as a flame passing from candle to candle, that is, from the arrested configuration of the modes in one generation to its exact duplication in another generation. And nirvana was revealed with the extinguishing or blowing out of this transgenerational flame. (Though judging from the Buddha's estimation of nirvana, rebirth was more of a great conflagration feverishly feeding on configuration after configuration of the modes and laying waste to the generations.) Nirvana was also seen, significantly, as (resulting from) *sundering* or as freedom since the flame of identity was generated from the modes by a process of clinging **(upadana),** a process which induced a state of dependency; but certainly, also because the defining quality of *dukkha,* the affliction that nirvana relieved, was that of constraint.

The Buddha himself gives evidence of the oppressive nature of his Kshatriya identity. To the Brahman student Ambattha he declares that it was even more oppressive than the Brahman estate identity: "The Khattiya's best among those who value clan . . ."[17] In the Buddha's case very likely, since the Shakyas were a tribal people who lived on the outskirts of the contemporary Gangetic civilization, while the Brahmans historically occupied the center.

Though throughout the scriptures what we find are attacks on the Brahmans, the Buddha's own struggles were first with the Kshatriya identity which society had given him. We must remember that the Buddha left home seeking a greater honor and integrity than his Kshatriya role and identity offered, and found these qualities only as a Brahman. But the Buddha would have soon found out after leaving home (if not before) that it was the Brahman estate which was the upholder of his own Kshatriya identity, that it was in the interest of this class to uphold the entire status quo of estate identities. The subsequent line of the above verse, "He with knowledge and conduct is best of gods and men,"[17] gives testimony to the Buddha's victory over his estate and clan loyalties. We see this even more clearly in the Buddha's contacts, before and just after his enlightenment, with the five monks with whom he had been practicing austerities for six years. When the Buddha rejoined these ascetics after his enlightenment, his first communication to them was that they not call him after his clan name of Gautama: "Call me not after my private name, for it is a rude and careless way of addressing one who has become an *Arhat.*"[18]

As a Kshatriya, the Buddha was constantly assailed with accusations from the Brahmans of his own blood impurity, that is, of having the blood of the enslaved Dravidian Sudras; the Brahmans claimed to be the "fairest" of all the estates (M II no. 93). Of course, in the scriptures this occurs only after the Buddha's enlightenment, but it would have been a reality all along. This bloodline or 'racial' conflict, this exclusion which must have been an affront, led him to search for the validity of identity. In the *Sutta Nipata* he declares his conclusion:

For what has been designated name and clan in the world is indeed a mere name. What has been designated here and there has arisen by common assent.

The false view of the ignorant has been latent for a long time. Only the ignorant tell us that one becomes a brahman by birth.[19]

The Buddha had finally seen through the Brahmans' veil of absolutism. The Brahmans had taught that one's birth identity was unchangeable in one's lifetime. One carried it to the grave. It was only in that nether realm between death and rebirth that change could occur depending on what one's conduct had been while one was still sentient. But the Buddha was never so submissive or gullible as to trust in such an unsupported means. He wanted and sought his salvation "in this very life." And this salvation was the vision of conditional origination. This doctrine was never the metaphysical one that it has come to be, but arose out of the context of social identity, and it was here that it had its most pertinent application, it was here that were realized its greatest possibilities for self-transformation. The Buddha goes on to say in the above that it is solely *action* which determines all social identity, including that of the estates which were assigned by birth. It is an unrefutable fact, then, that the 'rebirth' that rational conduct (the Eightfold Way) released one from was that which defined one's blood-identity.

When the Buddha rejected the atman he rejected an outmoded system of identity, and substituted an extremely noncategorical one. Referring to the five modes of karma or action which defines oneself—the body, expression, impression, configurations and entrancement—he noted that,

One should understand according to reality and true wisdom: This does not belong to me; this am I not; this is not my Ego.

Just as one calls hut the circumscribed space which comes to be by means of wood and rushes, reeds and clay, even so we call body the circumscribed space that comes to be by means of bones and sinews, flesh and skin.[20]

The Buddha was not dealing with an abstract 'self,' but with the very real identities of clan and estate. Why did he reject his Gautama-clan and Kshatriya identities? And why did such a noncategorical view of himself seem appropriate? The answer could only be that both of these identities, being based on blood and so static, had become irrelevant. The Buddha was fully aware of the profuse interbreeding of the various blood classes when he noted how unlikely it was, given one's long line of descent, to find anyone to whom one was not related (S II 89). Himself a product of interbreeding, the Buddha must have felt the inadequacy of the unilateral Kshatriya identity. And so he rejected this, which was to him a birth identity, and asserted his equal claim to a Brahman identity but chose to base this latter not on blood but on virtue. The Buddha had thus succeeded in escaping rebirth, that indulgence in, and the definition of oneself by, blood lineage and birthright.

It makes perfect sense now why the Buddha's nirvana was "unborn." It was simply not based on birthright. It was also unconditioned. Unlike the consciousness of the common person it was not an *entrancement* with the five modes. It was not confined to, and did not take as its basis, particular configurations of the modes, particular forms of the eye, ear, nose, etc. So the enlightened Buddha could not be identified. The incomprehensibility ascribed to nirvana does not stem from the nature of nirvana itself, but from the misunderstanding of the social phenomenon that nirvana gave release from.

The Brahmans' atman was unanalysable, undifferentiated and immutable. But so was the Buddha's nirvana. The difference was that the contemporary Brahmans sought these as intrinsic properties of the five modes, and the Buddha did not. The Brahmans' atman could never be "Unborn, Unoriginated, Uncreated, Unformed" since it was indistinguishable from the five modes which were themselves "the born, the originated, the created, the formed."[21] But in rejecting the five modes as a basis for identity—that is, in rejecting a blood-identity—the Buddha had resorted to an "Unborn, Unoriginated, Uncreated, Unformed."

The Buddha's nirvana was such a fundamental reality that not even the positive karma of virtue conditioned it. In other words, his rejection of the five modes was so complete, so uncompromising that he would refuse to allow even virtue to be the foundation, the justification for this rejection. This was a most remarkable thing, and its profound implications can easily elude us. Virtue, that purest and most innocent of human attributes (bar none, it would seem) was a paltry second best to the Buddha's nirvana. It was the only means (through the Eightfold Way) that nirvana could be reached, and yet even it had to be left outside the door (so to speak) of this sublime sunderance. It was truly a profound realization that the rejection (by way of the process of *anatta)* of the socially imposed identity did not need virtue, the good, in order to justify itself, and that it existed independently of, and even before the good. The Buddha realized immediately on that night beneath the Bodhi tree that this removal of his to an assurance preceding virtue was the consummation of the moral life, and that it was this that all the great sages of the past had achieved.

This utter betrayal of clan and estate identities was the centerpiece of the Buddha's awakening. His former allegiance to these identities and his rebellion against the accepted superiority of the Brahmans (with their vested interest in the continuance of his own Kshatriya identity) must have been fierce. It is interesting to note that the Brahmans themselves still continued to call the Buddha after his clan name. One cannot deny that the Buddhist canonical writings contain a great deal of anti-Brahman sentiment. Modern practitioners of Buddhism have neglected this fundamental aspect of the dharma. And with the inevitable amplification of the personage of the Buddha the Pali scriptures often soften what can only be the extreme ethnocentricity of the Kshatriyas and the Buddha's own Shakya clan—an ethnocentricity reinforced, no doubt, by the social preeminence of the Brahmans.

We can gauge the Buddha's rebelliousness from the legend of the holy man's prediction at the time of the Buddha's birth. The Buddha's life was said to have two possible outcomes: as a temporal ruler or redeemer. These two careers are juxtaposed in the legend because they are so opposed. This legend could hardly just depict an occult ceremony, but must express two very strong currents in the real emotional life of the Buddha. Born as a Kshatriya, the career choice of a philosopher or world redeemer would have been perceived unlikely for the Buddha, I should think. So that it must have been, instead, the implicit Brahmanic opposition to the early inclination to this career choice which would have reinforced in the Buddha the alternative of a world ruler or emperor. At any rate, at some time in his life, rule by force—that is, the career of a world conqueror, in other words, an emperor—must have seemed like a viable means to self-development and to righting the wrongs of his society. Such a career would, of course, have reinforced his own clan and Kshatriya identities, and very possibly at the expense of the Brahmans, since the Buddha would then have diverted the later philosophical disagreement with the Brahmans into the arena of military action.

The revolutionary nature of the dharma can also be seen in the story of the Buddha's hesitation on revealing his new understanding. The real reason for this must have been the clear possibility of Brahman hostility, for the Buddha certainly could not have been oblivious to the threat that his doctrine of **anatta** (nonidentity) presented to their social status. This doctrine went to the heart of Brahman theology and undermined their very notions of themselves.

So it was the renouncing of this clinging to his own social identity and the renouncing of hostility towards the social eminence of the Brahman estate that would have provided the Buddha with his great quenching or extinction:

[I]t is not from the standpoint of the attainment of unexcelled knowledge-and-conduct that reputation based on birth and clan is declared . . . But those who are enslaved by such things are far from the attainment of the unexcelled knowledge-and-conduct, which is attained by abandoning all such things![22]

In his twenty-ninth year the Buddha had walked away from his Shakya community and Kshatriya role to become an ascetic, but it would take him all of six years to truly break the allegiance to their identity in him.

★

The Buddha rejected his Kshatriya identity and asserted his claim to the highest identity within his society, that of a Brahman. But the Buddha's supreme achievement was to claim this identity not on the basis of blood (which he could have done), but through conduct. Even the Brahmans agreed that one became a true Brahman only by conduct and wisdom, and not by birth. The Brahmans agreed because this was the core teaching of the *Upanishads*. And a revolutionary teaching at that. For this was the means by which the society's earlier racial mixing was accommodated. A polarized society was created with the Aryan migrations into northern India. The Aryans consisted of warriors (Kshatriyas), priests (Brahmans) and commoners (Vaisyas). The priests were the designated caretakers and exemplars of their common cultural heritage. It was this ideal which the conquering Kshatriyas would, in time, have proclaimed as the common heritage of the whole society, even of the native populations. This might have been done because the invaders wanted to cease conflict with the original inhabitants or extend their control over the entire region. Over time, though, as the original Aryan heritage became more and more crossbred with the culture and biology of the darker natives, this revolutionary position would meet with increasing opposition, till the Brahmans would assert again the validity of bloodline. But by then the gulf between the Kshatriyas and their priests had irretrievably widened, for the warriors would have opened up much more completely to the wider society. And the more insular priesthood would have claimed superiority to the Kshatriyas on the basis of their designated function as upholders of an original Aryan heritage. The Kshatriyas (warriors and rulers), who had once been at one with their priests (the Brahmans) and had given over the safekeeping of their common ideal to the Brahmans, now found themselves estranged from this ideal. In one sense, the priesthood was a landless minority which, playing upon the sympathies of the ruling class had usurped the original common ideal. After such a long time the priests had, in effect, commandeered the Aryan migrations. They had fully succeeded in pacifying the warrior arm of the migrations. It was this schism that the Buddha was bridging when as a birthright Kshatriya he reasserted his Brahman identity.

We are in fact told in the *Upanishads* that the ones who first possessed the knowledge of reincarnation were the Kshatriyas.[23] This most definitely referred to a preoccupation with *genealogy,* certainly a natural concern of royalty. But even more. It could only have been that it was first within the Kshatriya estate that miscegenation with the slave Sudras had necessitated established definitions of racial purity, that is, *the number of generations of Aryan ancestry which was required before someone whose heritage contained Sudra blood could be considered again a Kshatriya.* As the class which produced the kings, this would seem to be a necessity. The Buddha himself notes in the *Digha Nikaya* (I 98–99) the very stringent ancestral requirements of the Kshatriyas. But it would be the Brahmans who would elevate this racial definition to a religion, transcending its racial context. It was the requirement of blood purity which over time would give rise to the religious practice of purification of identity (atman). Understandably, the necessity for racial purification had reached the more insular priesthood only after the warrior estate. But though late in coming, this practice would find its most enthusiastic following among the Brahmans. To the Brahmans, everyone's identity or atman was seen to be in a state of reincarnation or contamination. Only after rigorous moral and meditative practices could it be purified and so identified with Brahma, the universal identity. Of course, the Brahmans, as priests, defined the purified atman in terms of themselves. At first, this would not have been a problem, for both estates were in agreement. And the truth was that the Brahmanic system did transcend the racial context by defining a moral basis, a definition which allowed someone without the required amount of Aryan ancestry to assert the universal Brahma identity; though, of course, this was really a 'mulatto' religion, for very rarely, if at all, could a full-blooded Sudra practice in it, let alone attain to its goal of Brahma identity. It was the control of this philosophy which would give the Brahmans the greater leverage in the subsequent competition between the estates. Only then, when the moral basis of the Brahmanic system was abandoned and the racial context reasserted, and with the Kshatriyas finding themselves on the receiving end of the Brahmans' racial contempt, that they would seek, in Buddhism (and Jainism), to acquire their own religious expression of this racial context.

In this regard, the Buddha started out with certain basic assumptions of Brahmanism—the orthodox religious language of the day. One of these was that the appellation 'Brahman' designated the highest moral attainment in human society. This was the reason why the Buddha denied a rebirth causality to the Brahman but allowed it for others. To the Buddha, a Brahman was one who had achieved the extinction—the void or emptiness—of nirvana. Anything less than this total extinction was atman—identity, soul—and thus was intergenerational, reborn, a product of samsara. The Buddha denied that the positive (that is, a Brahman) is subject to rebirth, an intergenerational identity. It was only a negative impulse that underwent rebirth. And the Buddha did not see one's social status—or estate, however low—as necessarily being morally negative. Yet, to the Buddha, rebirth did occur. Now we can see that what the Buddha was really talking about with the doctrine of rebirth was our own notion of racial and ethnic identity. For with rebirth defined as *the transgenerational self-*

75

entity of a blood-identity, we can accommodate both the Buddha's insistence on the conditionality of all life and his acceptance that one did indeed receive a negative impulse from a previous generation. The negative impulse from a previous life was a blood-identity. And it was within this 'racial' or intergenerational identity that the Buddha saw all evil as occurring. To the Buddha, rationality could not support this identification with the past.

To the Brahmans the atman traveled the full spectrum of moral life, from negative to positive, from the greatest evil to the highest moral accomplishment of Tathagata—the Thus traveled (to Enlightenment), from the deepest blood-identity to the farthest individualism. The Brahmans defined the atman by the positive end of the spectrum, the Buddha defined it by the negative end. And to the Buddha the negative always produced the negative and the positive always produced the positive. So that the atman, agreed by both the Brahmans and the Buddha to be first encountered as negative, to the Buddha this atman could never become positive, never become Tathagata or Brahman. Are these two positions irreconcilable? No. For the Buddha was dealing with *causality.* And as far as causality went the negative could never produce the positive. But the Brahmans were not dealing with the mechanism of causality. They were dealing with a *structural* model of morality. Viewed structurally, the atman could be freed from its negative encumbrances and imbued with the positive, as indeed the Buddha claimed for the Bodhisattva.

The sticking point for the Buddha was that the Brahmans insisted that the moral continuum itself possessed a reality independent of its negative or positive designations. Thus the Brahmans believed that the atman, way up on the negative end of the spectrum, continued to be its essential positive self. The atman possessed its positive essence no matter how much it was overwhelmed by its antithesis, no matter how much it was negated. The truth is that this property of unconditionality within a self-entity was retained by the Buddha, but now it was a property of the Bodhisattva. No matter how far the Bodhisattva was thrust into

76

samsara—no matter how many cycles of rebirth he had accumulated—his nirvana was still guaranteed. So one system was merely a transformation of the other. There is no reason, also, why one cannot define the self-quality of the positive atman as Tathagata, for both definitions associate a self-entity with an unconditionality (nirvana in the case of the Bodhisattva, the absolute reality of Brahma in the case of the atman). The real point of contention was, instead, the association of the atman with bloodline and birthright. So what the Buddha's doctrine of **anatta** denied was not the atman as 'Self associated with an unconditioned,' but 'Self associated with bloodline,' that is, salvation as an intergenerational identity. The concept of the Bodhisattva was indeed free of the association with bloodline, and to be true his nirvana was always a potentiality, while the popular notion of the atman was that it existed even in an immoral character. The Buddha refused to believe that the ultimate goal of the holy life could coexist with its antithesis of rebirth. It was this consummation-in-potentiality, this positive-in-the-negative, that was so repugnant to the Buddha.

Given our definition of the atman it is obvious that something does continue even after the destruction of the five modes: this is their *identity,* which is a complete reflection or homunculi of these modes (from which it is detachable), and which finds a home in future generations. While the Buddha saw this *identity* as a thoroughly negative phenomenon, the Brahmans saw it as only superficially so. It was this 'self' which was erroneously thought in the Buddha's time to exist behind consciousness. This was not such a primitive notion, though, for it is still held by the vast majority of present humanity. (Consider, for instance, the notion in the United States of America that a person with a mere one percent African ancestry and ninety-nine percent Caucasian ancestry nevertheless has an inborn 'black' identity.) The opposite of this is the character of the Tathagata which is independent of all the modes and bears no reflection of them.

It is clear that though the *identity* bore the stamp of the five modes, it did not preserve or contain them in reality. Which was why the Buddha could claim the existence of a transgenerational effect (rebirth) but no content to this effect (nothing which was reborn). Though the *identity* of an individual bore the stamp of his consciousness or feeling or body or whatever, this identity taken up by an individual in a future generation did not impart a full-blown consciousness or feeling or body, etc., to this new individual. His five modes were always (at least) an equal result and function of the present life. The orthodox view in the Buddha's time, though, was that this identity did in fact provide the consummate form of the previous life's five modes to the individual in whom it found a new home. Obviously this identity did significantly determine the five modes of its new host. The Buddha, however, thought the extent to which it did *not* determine its host's five modes equally significant. To one way of thinking, the identity was the fully realized form of the five modes, while to the other it was a mere shell or imprint (and always ill-fitting) of these modes. We see, of course, how these two views reinforced their respective proponents. To the Brahmans, obsessed with blood purity, the view that the identity was the already fully realized individual, was nothing less than their lifeblood. Such a view, though, was invalidated by the Buddha's (openness to his) heritage of mixed blood. Either blood-identity, Brahman or Kshatriya, would be inconsistent with his five modes.

But before acquiring the character of Tathagata, the Buddha would go in search of this *identity* or spirit-form of the five modes. He would not find it. But what exactly was it that the Buddha did not find? The atman was not the same for everyone. The moral value of the Buddha's atman had caused it to be reborn as a Kshatriya, in the Brahmans' scheme of things a less than perfect form. And in the blood-based theology of the day a Kshatriya would have had to wait for the actual process of rebirth to occur just for the chance of achieving the perfect form of the atman, which was found only in Brahman social status. The Buddha's revolutionary move was to short-circuit this process by employing the discarded criterion of moral character to define the highest

78

status within the society. So through moral discipline the Buddha declared himself to be a Brahman, a word which everyone, including the Kshatriyas, agreed denoted the most desirable human character. So to answer our earlier question: what the Buddha did not find in himself was any evidence of a Kshatriya pattern of his five modes—of his body, expression, impression, configurations and entrancement—a pattern which the Kshatriyas themselves accepted as secondary. Attributed a subordinate moral identity (atman) as birthright, the Buddha had never grown into it, but above it. Of course, he could not then have found the subordinate identity in himself! He could, however, be a Brahman, for this was defined as singularly positive, and was the only fitting designation for the stature to which the Buddha had grown. Most others, though, accepting the subordinate identities of the Kshatriya, husbandman and servant estates, knew the 'reality' of the atman.

Quite frankly, a Brahman could have admitted that the reason the Buddha did not find his atman was because this had indeed become identified with the universal Brahma; that only the inferior manifestations of the atman—in Kshatriya, Vaisya and Sudra estate identity—had a separate and discernible existence. Buddhist scripture does indeed give many instances of Brahman acceptance of the Buddha as a Brahman, though in the social reality that prevailed, one was not really supposed to find the purified atman but an atman commensurate with one's estate. But using this Brahmanic language, that would mean that the atman was always negative. It only became positive when it was subsumed in the universal Brahma, that is, when it did not exist. But isn't this what the Buddha was saying? This is not a far cry from the teaching of the *Upanishads*. What then had gone wrong? Obviously it was the exaltation of the atman as a separate entity, before it had been dissolved in the universal Brahma, a practice which could only be deleterious, for the atman in its own right was always negative. But such a tendency, and language, was begun even in the *Upanishads*. The atman was praised and attributed the property of unconditionality as a (seemingly) separate entity to the universal

Brahma, a separation which could only mean that the atman was not subsumed in Brahma and so was inferior, but what was no doubt implicitly understood and meant by the Upanishadic sages was the dissolution of the atman in Brahma. So it was the attributing of the properties of the universal Brahma to the unsubsumed and inferior atman—a blood-identity—which put the Buddha at odds with the Brahmans. Intended to be dissolved in Brahma, the atman was arrested in this process and had acquired a life and devotion of its own, so that the finger pointing to the moon was taken for the moon itself.

What, then, was the nature of the atman? What was the defining property of this identity? The prevailing notion was pretty commonsensical: the identity (atman) preserved the very content of, for example, consciousness, so that one could actually retrieve the knowledge that was collected in a previous life. The Buddha outright rejected this. In place of this identity he substituted a mechanical *causality*. But this, I maintain, is the very nature of identity; causality is equivalent to identity. The Buddha did not say so, though. He had simply replaced the atman with a mechanical rebirth. But we have already noted the reason for his rejection of the contemporary atman even as negative (causal) reality: it was the ascribing to it, as the five modes, of the property of unconditionality; a property, of course, which could never exist within the causality of rebirth. But its *illusion* certainly could, and would necessarily exist within the causality of suffering. It is the illusion of the property of unconditionality as a function of the five modes which defines a blood-identity. This illusion is also none other than the mechanism of rebirth. So that it was the property of unconditionality (intrinsic to Brahma) but applied to the five modes, which made the monk, Sati (M I no. 38), assert that consciousness was "independent." The chain of conditional origination showed that rebirth did, indeed, provide a causal impulse to consciousness, that is, in contrast to arising as a full-blown reality as Sati erroneously believed. The Buddha reprimanded Sati for holding the view that consciousness continued through "rebirth." It did not, certainly not as a full-blown reality. But its causal impulse did continue. What Sati did not believe in was the conditional origination of his illusion, that the *identity* of consciousness was *not* consciousness. The reflection of the five modes in an identity (with its illusion of unconditionality) was not a consummate reflection. It was not a complete duplicate, not a clone. It was a selective reflection, rather like an x ray. It was the *causal dimension* of the five modes that it preserved; for it is obvious that the identity of the five modes does indeed provide a causal impulse to the future life in which it finds a home. So causality (rebirth) did have a form, and that form was identity. The degenerate atman (blood-identity) did exist as causal–rebirth reality, not as unconditioned reality as the Brahmans' claimed. So what were extinguished in nirvana were the five modes as a *reflection* in identity.

An identity projected backwards and forwards indefinitely allows for no conditionality. It is impulsive, automatic. Its past is equal to its present, is equal to its future. It was rightly seen as a terrifying prospect, prisonlike and claustrophobic. This mechanism lay at the foundation of a static society. To the Brahmans' credit, they did recognize this, and so upheld (in theory at least) that anyone, no matter the estate he was born into, could become a Brahman once he had succeeded in escaping the insularity of identity. But of course the Brahmans were Brahmans whether or not they themselves had escaped the infinite projection of identity. As the guardians of the ancient Upanishadic wisdom they had assured themselves, superficially indeed, of this sublime liberation by also defining it as theirs by birthright. What they succeeded in doing was contradictory to say the least: blood-identity was extinguished in its very continuation.

The inexorable transmigration of identity from the inconceivable past to an indefinite future was indeed the closing of the mind and the stagnation of society. It was this tyranny of identity that the Buddha struggled against. He found his salvation in an awareness of the conditionality of his life and society. While the Brahmans saw a permanent soul infusing the five modes, the Buddha saw these as composed entirely of action (karma). The Buddha's world was made up not of particles and their aggregates, but of action and its five modalities of body, expression, impression, configurations and entrancement. Even for the very physical body the Buddha recognized as its first reality the action-quality of change, of impermanence. He referred to the eye, ear, nose, tongue, body and mind as "old karma."[27] Action was the all pervading fabric of the world, from the unreflective impulse ("new karma") which caused suffering to the rational conduct which produced the character of the Brahman with which one experienced the unconditioned:

> Thus the wise, seeing conditional origination, knowing the fruit of action, see this action as it really is.
>
> By action the world goes on; by action people go on. Beings have action as their bond, as the linch-pin is the bond of a chariot as it goes along.[28]

This was the vision that nirvana provided, the extinction of *identity,* the replacing of a solidity by fluidity, of a discrete reality by dynamism. This property of conditionality, of flux, was never limited by the Buddha to just the human form. The Brahmans had always seen the atman or soul as infusing all of phenomenal reality. In rebirth one's atman could infuse any plant or animal and even inanimate objects. So the Buddha always made it a point to extend the rejection of the atman to all forms "internal or external . . . far or near."

The Buddha rejected a structural model of the self for a functional model. Though the atman was not supposed to possess any corporeal qualities, it was a mirror image of the corporeal self. And in the eyes of the Buddha the definition of the atman included the bodily sphere, for in rejecting the atman the Buddha rejected the corporeal self as an integral part. On the other hand, moral causality—the functional model of the self—did not in the slightest resemble the "fathom-long carcass" which obeyed its operation. The relationship of moral causality—the positive in the positive,

82

the negative in the negative—to bodily form, is rather like that of the helical DNA molecule, which, though containing all of the information for the body's development, does not in the least resemble the body. Or, one might think, the relationship is rather like the Copernican model of the solar system. This model—of the planets revolving around the sun, and the moon around the earth—contradicts common sense. The Ptolemaic model—of the sun and planets and moon all revolving around the earth—is the common-sense model. The atman and blood-identity, like the Ptolemaic system, are commonsense models of the self. Moral causality, though—the functional model of the self—like the Copernican model, forces us to look beneath the surface. And so the Copernican model of the solar system, more commensurate with reality, replaced the commonsense Ptolemaic model. And the perception of the functional model of a moral causality extinguishes the commonsense models of atman and birth identity. This is nirvana, the extinction of the false selves of atman and blood. With their extinction, the atman and blood-identity are seen for what they really are: illusions, mirages. Only the inexorable flux and flow of causality remains—the positive in the positive, the negative in the negative.

The agent of moral causality is *identity*. Causality is equivalent to an intergenerational identity—rebirth. When the Buddha denied the existence of the atman, what he was really denying was that, with the atman defined as an intergenerational identity, one could at the same time see it as encompassing that understanding which perceives the mechanism of rebirth and is its opposite. Here again is met that contradiction of the Brahmans that blood-identity was extinguished in its very continuation; a snake swallowing itself since causality was always negative and the direct opposite of rationality.

To avoid this contradiction the Buddha outright rejected the atman, not bothering to see it as having positive and negative aspects (as the Brahmans saw it), and instead retained rebirth as an incontrovertible negative. The Buddha simply refused to layer this negativity with the bipolar atman. The positive, to the Buddha, was always widely separated from the negative. Still, as we have noted, the two systems are interchangeable. And in the Tathagata (the Thus-traveled) we have the equivalent of the positive atman, for the Tathagata before enlightenment, as the Bodhisattva, traversed through innumerable cycles of birth and death before finally arriving at the liberation of nirvana. This was likewise the journey of the Brahmans' atman. So here again we must conclude that the Buddha's contention with the Brahmans was not in the realm of the metaphysical, but in the Brahmans' insistence on their blood-identity as being compatible with the moral life.

Identity is the central concern of Buddhism. This could only have been possible if it was also the central concern of the Buddha's life. The solution to the constraints and questions of his estate and clan identities was the rejection of these. But to validly reject that identity which history and society had set for him through his mere 'existence' or birthright, the Buddha had to reject all forms of blood-identity, "all inclination to the vainglory of I and mine."[24] The Brahmans still continued to treasure their transgenerational atman and its Brahman identity on the basis of birthright. But the Buddha, with his enlightenment, had entered that knowledge for which (as the *Upanishads* noted) birthright "Brahmans and Kshatriyas are but food, and death itself a condiment."[25] The Buddha had attained to that knowledge of which the birthright Brahmans only professed to know:

That bhikkhu who has not found any essence in existences, as one searching among fig-trees (does not find) a flower . . .
That bhikkhu in whom there are no angers inwardly, and (who) has gone beyond the state of (being reborn in) such and such an existence, leaves this shore and the far shore as a snake leaves its old worn-out skin.[26]

Though the Buddha had tried to redefine what a Brahman was, in the end the word 'Brahman' was successfully monopolized by the birthright Brahmans, who were able to hold on to its definition as a blood-identity. The Buddha resorted to various other choices to denote the attainment he advocated, words that were not already appropriated by any group or school of thought. However, at least one of these had similar origins in social status and lineage as the word 'Brahman,' but which the Buddha was able to wrest from the birthright prerequisites of the Brahmans. This was the word *aryan* (of high rank, noble), a word which was originally used by the conquering Kshatriyas, Brahmans and Vaisyas to refer exclusively to themselves.

Conclusions

A structural model of the self is not necessarily erroneous, possibly just inadequate. What is erroneous is when this model is given a fixed and immutable configuration, and so becomes affiliated with bloodline and birthright—the defining property of primitive society—as the Brahmans' atman had become. Thus the Brahmans reverted to the primitive life of sacrifice that the atman, in its original definition equivalent to 'Tathagata,' had lifted them out of. It was knowledge of Brahma–atman that defined Indian civilization. By the time of the Buddha, though, the Brahmans were enmeshed once again in the irrationality of ritual. The Brahmans could have continued as an isolated breeding population, other nonmoral circumstances allowing, but their position became untenable when they appropriated the society's moral system in this regard.

It was because it had become contaminated with the blood of clan and estate that the Buddha rejected the word 'atman.' By the time of the Buddha, the atman was no longer an individual self- or ego-entity, but a collective phenomenon—of clan, lineage, estate, birthright. It was this degeneration that the Buddha was reacting to —this was the larger social reality—and not the original, positive reality of the atman. The Buddha would take this original Vedic wisdom—then a matter of mere theory to the Brahmans—to its greatest heights, its logical and practical conclusion. The atman and its essential quality of individualism were betrayed by the Brahmans with the antithesis of birthright. Which is the reason that Brahmanism could not travel: it was mired in the blood of lineage and clan. Buddhism, on the other hand, was the ideal packaging of an original Upanishadic wisdom. These were two divergent currents of Vedic thought, one the blood-based salvation of Brahmanism, the other the pure rationality of Buddhism.

India's subsequent paralysis and decay were never the result of the Buddha's doctrine of nonviolence (as some have thought). India was wounded long before the Buddha. As the early Upanishadic knowledge lost its meaning, there was a proliferation of allegiance to blood-identity in the four estates and clan, and later in caste. But the atman's web of discrete existences did not stop with the individual; it reached into the larger social and nonsocial realm. It was this wound of blood-identity that caused India's eternal stagnation and rot. And it was blood-identity that the Buddha sought to cure India of. This was the purpose of his doctrine of **anatta,** which refuted the existence of identity either in subject or object phenomena:

> "How can we know, Sir, how can we see, that in this consciousness-endowed body and externally among all outer objects, there is no I-ness, no mine-ness, no underlying tendency to conceit?"
>
> "Whatsoever body . . . feeling . . . perception . . . mental activities . . . consciousness, Radha, past, future or present, internal or external, gross or subtle, inferior or superior, far or near, is looked upon as 'This is not mine,' 'I am not this,' 'This is not myself,'—in this manner it is seen according to actuality with perfect wisdom. Thus knowing, thus seeing, in this consciousness-endowed body and externally among all outer objects there is no I-ness, no mine-ness, no underlying tendency to conceit."[29]

The Buddha rejected identity (the atman) as an interpretive/explanatory tool in analyzing phenomena. This is laid out in the discourse on the Four Foundations of Mindfulness (M I no. 10). Here the disciple is instructed to perceive the body relative only to itself, the body in terms only of the body; expression relative only to itself, in terms only of expression; and similarly entrancement and configurations. In contrast to the leaving off of observation which occurs in the eight stages of the yogic cultivation of self-absorption, the Buddha proposed the careful observation of the processes and phenomena of the body and mind. This had a very specific purpose. Thereby the disciple convinced himself of the unreality of the atman, of an unconditioned property belonging to sentience.

The Brahmans' great irrationality (and the irrationality of all those who believe in a soul) was to uphold that the supreme goal of the moral life existed in all its completeness at the same time that it was defined by its antithesis of rebirth, a transgenerational identity. What this achieved in practice was the exaltation of blood-identity and birthright, and so relieved one of the necessary effort to achieve that contingent self or ego (the Thus-traveled) which is the only true consummation of the moral life. And so the Buddha's incessant prescription was for the destruction of the infinite projection of identity through the recognition of the impermanence of all its underlying modes. Knowledge *(vijja)* was in fact defined by the Buddha in the *Samyutta Nikaya* as the awareness of impermanence:

"How knowing, Sir, how seeing is ignorance *(avijja)* abandoned and understanding *(vijja)* produced?"
"By knowing and seeing the impermanence of the eye . . . ear . . . nose . . . tongue . . . body . . . mind . . . mind-objects . . . mind-consciousness . . . mind-contact . . . And whatever arises conditioned by mind-contact, felt as pleasant or painful or neutral—by knowing and seeing the impermanence of that also, ignorance is abandoned and understanding is produced."[30]

The religious doctrine of rebirth was just a manifestation of the transgenerational identities of clan and estate which pervaded the society. The ancients conceptualized it in a completely literal way as 'repeated birth'; as indeed it was! A true Brahman was purebred, that is, *repeatedly born in the same line* for seven generations. Rebirth was the replication of oneself in a future generation as true to form as possible, to do which one needed a spouse as close in lineage as possible. Hence the system of clans and estates and later castes. The fallen atman represented that selective process which human populations have performed upon themselves preceding even the domestication of plant and animal species when a similar process came into play. The ancients failed to recognize the real basis of their belief in transmigration, but without a doubt their moksha was the release from the ties of blood. This would have been true for the Buddha as well as the sages of the *Upanishads*.

The great ideal of the *Upanishads* was detachment from the blood-identity of estate. It was the constraint of blood-identity that one freed the atman from and united it with Brahma, the universe. The devout Brahman pursued this goal as the last phase of his life, basically in his retirement years. But even before the time of the Buddha this tail-end practice of the dharma was no longer tenable. Renouncers left home for the homeless life at any stage of life—in middle age, in young manhood, even in youth. Could this have been because by the time of the fourth life-stage the would-be renouncer had enjoyed all there was to enjoy in his estate identity, making renunciation superfluous, even hypocritical? For before leaving home for the homeless life at this late stage one would have produced progeny, and in so many other ways secured the continuation of the very rebirth which one was leaving home to destroy. This, quite possibly, would have been one of the reasons why renunciation had become, by the time of the Buddha, a lifetime career.

The Buddha could be right and the Brahmans could be right at the same time because they were both talking at cross-purposes. The Buddha was referring to the Brahmans' blood-identity as the practical face of their atman. To the Brahmans their contemporary atman was always the original atman realized through moral conduct. The Brahmans refused to see their social condition as being relevant to the realization of the atman. But it was. The atman of farthest individualism and self-assurance was lost to them. That was why the Buddha rejected the Brahmans' atman and proclaimed a contingent character obtained through moral conduct—the Tathagata or Thus-traveled. The Brahmans' atman was the direct opposite of this since one did not obtain it through development, but automatically through birth as Brahman estate identity, Kshatriya estate identity, Vaisya estate identity, Sudra estate identity.

Though it took a long time, in the end the Brahmans won the war for the hearts of India, for Buddhism did eventually disappear from the subcontinent (until very recently). And the Brahmans were able to reassert their exclusive claim to legitimacy. The original blood-lineage context of the dharma was lost in the societies (possibly more ethnically homogeneous) to which the Buddha's message had migrated. This is probably a major reason why the *material* basis of the dharma was never discovered till now.

Human society has always possessed a stubborn tendency to see reality through the distortion of identity and a distaste for its naked truth. But the blood-lineage basis of the dharma was never in the first place explicit to the ancients. It had always been a metaphysical displacement. This was a carry-over from prehistory where the complex web of human social identities—clan, tribe, moiety, age-group, gender, etc.—were displaced outward unto the nonhuman organic and nonorganic environment. This was the process that had produced the nature deities and culture of animism of aboriginal society. The Brahmans themselves saw the atman existing not only within the human form but in all material forms. Even in modern industrial society this aboriginal displacement continues in the belief in 'encounters' with extraterrestrial beings and their spaceships. Such forms reflect the technological nature of modern society in the same way that the spirit world reflected the Buddha's own society.

One wonders, though, how the Buddha could have granted to the deities and spirit-forms that populated his world a greater reality than identity (the atman). If the atman was 'spiritual,' wouldn't this have put it in the same realm as the deities, and wouldn't the Buddha just as uncompromisingly have rejected the spirit world as he did the atman? The truth could only be that because the atman was *not* 'spiritual' and so not of the same class of phenomena as the deities, **anatta** did not apply in its comprehensiveness to the spirit world. The Buddha still ascribed a significant reality to this world, though it was as illusory as the atman. The reason for this must have been that while the atman with its manifestations in estate identity was a source of social constraint, the spiritual cosmology was not: everyone had equal access to it. The Buddha treated the spirit world in the same noncombative way that he did the trancelike meditation that was already so entrenched in the society: both these were attributed a lesser reality than that of the Arhat, the one liberated through moral discipline.

The ancients were never conscious of the direct dependence of the dharma on the society's blood-lineage context, but as long as this context remained in close proximity the dharma retained its full validity. But in time the dharma became estranged from its original context, and because it was not fully conscious in the first place, its loss was never really felt. I have retrieved this lost dimension and so hopefully saved an essential strand of Buddhist thought—that of rebirth—from irrelevancy. But this necessarily entailed invoking a level of dharma which both the Theravada and the Mahayana have become alienated from. This is the social and cultural context of the contemporary Indian society. We can detect in Buddhist scripture two distinct levels. One level deals with the system of estates and the Buddha's disagreements with the Brahmans. The other is a more abstract level, but it is really just a formularization of the cruder, material basis. But the Theravada paid a big price for this sanitized version of the dharma. They lost the language within which the nature of the Buddha's enlightenment finds clear and unambiguous expression.

The problem of dharma is lastly a problem of language. The sphere of reality that dharma covers may be divided into two segments: a *problem* field and a *solution* field. Of course, this corresponds to the dichotomy of samsara/nirvana. But the choice of words that translators employ (and that very likely exists in the original Pali, or at least *understood* to be denoted by the Pali), this choice of words ignores this 'fracture' in reality. So that an English translator will employ the indiscriminately encompassing word "consciousness" for the Pali **vinnana.** But **vinnana** is really part of that segment of reality defined as *problem.* But by using such a 'universal' term, that translator has denied himself the choice of a word, taken from the *solution* field, which is antithetical to **vinnana.** He has, indeed, 'painted himself into a corner.' We can certainly be assured that the Buddha, after his enlightenment which extinguished the five modes (including **vinnana**), was conscious! The solution to this obviously illogical state of affairs is a choice of words for the *problem* field that is more narrowly defined than their counterparts in the *solution* field. Thus I have used the word "entrancement" for the Pali **vinnana,** which allows us to describe the fact that indeed the Buddha was conscious after his enlighten-ment. This is a criterion I have employed throughout:

Problem field	*Solution* field
(atta) blood-identity	self
(bhavana) birthright	existence
(satto) kind	being
(tanha) compulsion	desire
(dhamma) tradition	phenomenon
(vinnana) entrancement	consciousness
(dukkha) constraint	suffering
(khandha) modes	aggregates
(sankhara) configurations	mental formations
(jati) rebirth	birth

In the conventional approach of the right column the only "extinc-tion" that can occur is one of physical destruction; while in the left column—the items of which may be seen as subsets of their counterparts in the right column—a *moral* extinction is certainly possible, and indeed desirable. These differing results are obtained because of the contrasting criteria which determine the columns. The left (unorthodox) column is defined in purely moral terms, while the right column is defined in physical (or amoral) terms. The difference between the left and right columns—that is, in going from the unorthodox interpretation to the orthodox—represents the semantic shift (in the *problem* field, a tendency to an indiscriminate invocation), that had occurred by the time the teachings of the Buddha were finally put into written form. This was probably done about three to four centuries after they were first spoken, and then on the island of Sri Lanka a thousand miles to the south, significantly insulated from the Aryan occupation and remaking of the Ganges basin.[31]

★

Perhaps it was the loss in social relevance of the concept of rebirth—the great anathema of the early Buddhists—which allowed the later Mahayana Buddhists to embrace so wholeheartedly in their ideal of compassion the social milieu that the Theravada turned away from. In any case, the moral tenacity of the Theravada tradition of renunciation had lost its sway for many, and the reverse practice of compassion took its place. Yet the Mahayana retained the central doctrine of **anatta**—the absence of a soul or underlying essence in reality. What this hypercompassion must have done was replace (as moral basis) a renunciation turned hollow when the significance of rebirth was lost, when in essence it was paid only lip service. Certainly one is convinced that this doctrine is of paramount importance only to the very earliest of Buddhists, not even the Theravadins. And with the Mahayana it played an even more insignificant and superfluous role. It would be this altered dharma—a renunciation reversed and a rebirth of little relevance—which would proliferate through the centuries.

Can one be enlightened without escaping the cycle of rebirths, that is, without escaping the transgenerational identity of blood? Is everything else merely "comfortable abidings in the here and now"?[32] Knowledge of one's former lives was an integral part of enlightenment (not only the stopping of future lives). What could this knowledge be but the *acknowledgment* of one's mixed (multiple-lineage) heritage? The Buddha, we are told, on the night of his enlightenment surveyed what was in effect his genealogy, and rejected the notion of an immutable transgenerational identity (thus putting an end to rebirth). The apprehension of this identity in oneself was a requirement of the dharma. One must have had it to escape it. Obviously the Buddha thought that everyone possessed this identity to a greater or lesser degree, for it was the destruction of this identity which was the dharma's singular purpose.

The ancients thought that it was the arising of a transgenerational identity which not only preceded but generated one's body, and so the extinction of this identity would destroy any further arising in future lives of a body for oneself with its inherent old age, sickness and death; though one must undergo this bodily decay for the last time in the body that had already arisen. But though one's transgenerational identity did indeed manifest itself in the womb— that is, at conception—and in a real birth and real body, for us moderns the actual old age, sickness and death that would occur no more with the realization of nirvana was a metaphysical one, one which occurred to the *identity* projected into the future. One may wonder just to what extent was the release from future old age, sickness and death also a metaphysical consolation to the ancients, since the dharma did not release them from the present (and what to us are the only real) old age, sickness and death. At any rate the nirvana or extinction in the present life for both the Buddha and us moderns is the ending of "greed, hate and delusion," those protecting sheaths of a blood-identity:

Now, in so far as the monk has realized the complete extinction of greed, hate and delusion, in so far is Nibbana realizable, immediate, inviting, attractive and comprehensible to the wise.[33]

In the scriptures what we find is the Buddha denouncing Brahman *social* identity. In the Ambattha Sutta of the *Digha Nikaya* we find Brahmans protesting that "Gotama is depreciating not only our color, but our ritual training and birth."[34] The Buddha was not a birthright Brahman. He was a Kshatriya. All of the estates, however, were the materializations of the same underlying entity, the atman. It was just that the Brahman was the exemplary identity, the theoretical potential of all the other estates. The Buddha was not concerned in denouncing the Kshatriyas who were the rulers and the owners of society's wealth. It was, instead, the Brahmans' unjustified claim to moral superiority that he found so objectionable. It was a moral or psychological oppression that he rebelled against. The Buddha refused to condescend to the presumed piety of the Brahmans.

In himself the Buddha did not have to reject Brahman identity. He was the less exemplary Kshatriya, and it was this material manifestation of atman that he had to reject. In denying the reality of the atman, the Buddha was denying the reality of his Kshatriya identity. But the Buddha did not specifically reject this identity. To do so and still to take on Brahman identity as he did could never be morally supported. He would be exchanging one blood-identity for another, exalting one over the other. This was the reason that he rejected only the atman in the atman–Brahma pair, for the atman was the common characteristic shared by all the estates. The Brahman identity which he claimed, he divorced from the blood reality of the atman and based it instead upon conduct.

In rejecting the atman the Buddha, in effect, rejected a 'racial' definition of self. The system of estates was indistinguishable from present-day racial identity. Marrying outside of one's estate destroyed one's identity, and so this was forbidden. This is the case with racial identity. Both identities, atman and race, have their origins in an inscrutable past. And it is this inscrutability, this irrationality, which lay at the foundation of the Buddha's contemporary society, and of society today. Both types of societies, then and now, are hierarchical to a great degree.

Those today who would practice the dharma and not equate race with atman, they miss the greatness of the dharma. Such people look for the atman, the soul, as a spiritual homunculi, a spiritual atom; but they look with the eyes of physical science. But modern science does not cater to the moral character of human life. So of course they do not find any atman, and they think that they have successfully rejected it. Modern science deals with the physical character of reality. The dharma deals with the moral character of reality. The atman is a moral entity, a moral construct. Its correct interpretation is *blood-identity*. That is the moral atom or homunculi of the world, the building block of all moral phenomena.

III
A West Indian Buddhism

The truth of constraint

1. On an exile shore among a broken people sit and wonder at your lot. If fate gave birth to you among a people so cast down as these, could you turn away? Among an orphan people, not born to institutions, whose lives are baseless, their dreams unable to soar, could you turn away to your salvation? From those who have no congregation of like minds, who in derision stand apart, could you rise above duty to know that unconditional sundering of the dark?

My island home was the place of greatest joy and the engendering of dizzying dreams. But an innocent inherits dreams and not the tolerance for bleak reality. And as a child in his dreams will embrace the world, a man grows up rooted, his identity accrued only with the loss of alternatives. Now older than all the players in your childhood myths, you are gone over. This life will not constitute itself. This turmoil cannot find a home in anyone. A house of cards, a paper man, pain draws you down, it draws you down.

2. See how artificial are all the faces, how ill-bred the conduct. A disfigured people abandoned on these shores to their own blundering devices. How unhappy you walk the streets of your captivity, how lost is your aim. At each turn you stumble and fall. How you writhe in agony, the victim of every vile fool. Could you turn away to your salvation? In swirling suffering you are bound. Their deep delusion blinds you. You are clawed by the cold hands of their pain. Could you turn away to your salvation?

Here for you there is only a dank and dusty corner of life. Only the drab, green youth, the frightening, encrusted age; only this incoherent experience with no view to achievement; only a deep exile; an ill-fitting exterior, an empty heart; a close, crowding, dark affection, a ghostly mien. From a hundred fated blows this life is hurt deeply. A gaping wound bleeds the heart and all desire is a cringing nerve. Could you turn away to your salvation?

3. When the springtime approaches near, there is the feeling of all possibilities, that a thousand worlds stand waiting. An unusual sun in late winter raises a hundred smells among mingling bodies and startles your mind along myriad paths, while sunlight in infinite ways conspires before your eyes. And along your lonely way girls' faces grip the mind, shine like the sun, all gold and light, auburn hair, pomegranate skin and dark, dark eyes. And you wonder, "Where do they go from here, these burnished vessels who draw man's burdened load and give him rest? who cut the thongs of his feverish love and set him free? to what magical world where eyes and hair and skin have mythic proportions?" But beyond your world these daughters of the sun live, while with you entrancing accents linger, here where youth has long since fled but no props for maturity been found. And so you cry, "O God! what is that world that love and family secure? that virtue binds? Where does it lie?" And still you ask yourself, "Did you ever really understand there are no guarantees in life, not even for what you most consider yourself, your body?" And this unusual day in the winter of the mind warms all but your frozen life.

4. So now, when the sun has gone out of the world and the laden curtain of night is drawn across the sky and dark shadows reach everywhere, now when your fever crackles and burns and pain swiftly approaches, where do you turn? To what arms do you run? Cold are the arms of disenchantment, shallow the walls of loneliness. Shod is this roof of pride, *raging* are these elements of craving. How to rebuild this life too raw, too much on end, too hurtful? What is this bleeding of the soul? Why this gushing hurt? What is this pining, this weariness and fainting, this dying? What

is this alarm and straining, this tearing and feverish vision: the filling of what form?

But when the night descends and the dark encloses, when the gloom enshrouds, and as the terror strikes and the fear transfixes, be brave, O heart. There is a certain nobility to a life that fights. The new sun in rising the eye may hold but the heart overflow. O pregnant, golden light with gift of a new day, give birth to a griefless world.

The truth of the cause of constraint

5. All things produce after their kind. As plant and animal species, so too moral entities. Joy, true to its nature, produces joy; and pain, always true to its nature, produces pain: the positive in the positive, the negative in the negative. This is fundamental rationality, the inexorable law which all the buddhas see:

It is not through that which is common, monks, that the sublime is realized. It is through the sublime that the sublime is realized.[1]

A lower value cannot displace a higher value. You cannot displace what you admire with what you pity and still continue to look up. You cannot displace joy with pain and still hope to find happiness. Never, in all the world, can you displace your heart with alienation and still find your way home.

The channel that your craving took was condescension. What you thought was your pain was really your compulsion: what you thought was the effect was really the cause. What you thought was responsible was really your salvation. You were shallow because you loved shallowness. You were false because you loved falseness. You became unfit because you condescended to the unfit.

6. Now I see the choice I have: a philosophy based on joy and desire or a philosophy based on pain and injury: the positive in the positive, the negative in the negative. One cannot find light in

darkness nor the positive in the negative. Understanding does not come through suffering. They are opposed as night and day. Understanding is clarity, rationality. Suffering is oppressive and impairing. To seek understanding in pain is like looking for clarity in darkness, like looking for a firm foothold in water. A firm foothold is found only on land, and clarity is found only in joy and happiness: the positive in the positive, the negative in the negative.

So do not think to yourself: "How can anyone understand my suffering? How can anyone replicate those years of agony, day upon day, moment by moment? How can I convey to another the experience of chronic pain?" For here lies the flaw in such thinking: understanding, which you wish to impart, does not arise from suffering. Understanding arises from itself, arises from clarity. Suffering retards understanding, stifles understanding, blocks it from ever arising. It is joy and happiness, but never pain, that you must look for in others to find a home for your understanding.

7. The positive and the negative are poles apart. To find one is to be without the other. You cannot get achievement through defeat, or joy through pain. You cannot dig a sore for its cure. Therein lies that inordinate desire which never finds its way home. It depends, then, on the premise. If you start out with pain you will only find pain. But if you start out with joy you will always find joy, no matter how much pain there is. And the premise of joy can exist in the greatest pain. For you cannot harvest "grapes from thornbushes" or "figs from thistles." How true it comes through! Pain does not bestow strength, pain bestows weakness. That is a law eternal. All my life all I have ever wanted was joy. But now I see how all my life I have celebrated pain, I have danced to pain, I sang to it, I feasted to it. I see clearly now the enemy I have lain with.

8. An alchemist of pain, I multiplied my dark ore like loaves of bread, ate and shared abundantly. Out of my heavy element I fashioned a universe of forms and decorated my life. I laid my founda-

tion and built my high walls brick upon brick and gave a home to my heart's desolation. I fenced my yard and locked in my enemy. I sowed my acre and reaped my bitter fruit. O! how staunch was my allegiance to my heart's abomination. How steadfast my defense of my own demise. How great was Mara's mockery then, as I labored at my tomb. How his laughter must have shook the high heavens. O, how painful was this householder's life, how confounding. Contented householder that I was, how many times did I shout for joy, "Here comes Mara once again in procession with his black priests going the round of rebirths!" How many times did I dole out my heart's treasures and take my fill of their rueful babble. How painful was this householder's life, how confounding.

9. All my life I have looked in my tiredness for strength, sought in my drowsiness for clear vision. How long it was to learn that patience is the germ around which the crystal of peace forms: the positive in the positive, the negative in the negative. Never could you displace virtue with suffering and still walk upon the path of Dharma. Where there is darkness there is no light. The solution is not found in the problem. When "*all configurations (of body and mind) are impermanent,*" where, then, is that underlying essence of existence? It is nowhere! When "*all configurations (of body and mind) are constraining,*" where, then, is that trancelike, euphoric Nirvana? It is nowhere! "*All traditions are without (transgenerational) identity.*"[2] There is no painless atman which goes through life unaffected by earthly existence. There is no unconditioned rationality. All rational morality is conditioned by earthly phenomena, arises from profane phenomena alone. Where, then, is the celestial, heavenly Buddha? He is nowhere!

10. Here in this body was your virtue accumulated. Here was your innocence safeguarded. Here was the only one who knew what beauty truly was. And yet you scorned and reviled it, you shunned it for another. The sinning mind you sided with. That foul abstraction was your lover. Poor body! This fair one you whipped, you kicked and stoned. What did it do to deserve such wrath?

Such a gentle one, so kind, so caring. Why did you denigrate it? Why did you throw it upon the dung heap? You covered your ears from its whispering, and when you heard its pleading voice you called it a liar. Its every move and impulse you thwarted. Till it ran aground in your self-destruction. Poor, poor body! What did it do to deserve such wrath? What did it ever do but store up your virtue? What did it ever do but gather your treasures, and when at last you returned repentant give it all up without a grudge—this the only concentration, this the only unity of mind, this precious heart nestled in the real body? Why did you stay away so long?

11. Mind is a colony of the outside and foreign. It is a colonial power which forces in upon one's original self. And then it pronounces its curse of 'body.' That is why you could never find your true self through mind. But there is a reason within the body, a rationality which can put an end to the mind's usurpation. This is the moral. For when a man is untrue in his body, how can his mind be truthful? When a man is truthful in his body, how can his mind be false? It is only when one recognizes the intrinsic virtue and integrity of body that one can recover original self and dispel the pain, humiliation and shame that are the mind's foul secretions.

So when the mind is racked with pain, when it turns to violence, and its views screech and hawk at the views of others, continue to treasure the body's reason: smile at others, be polite, be kind, forgive, show respect, be generous, admire the good in others: because this is your only highway of escape from the mind's pain. It is the body's reason which must displace the mind. Because if the body's reason is corrupted by the mind then you are surely on a runaway horse with no reins. If the body goes, you cannot turn yourself around again. It will be left to others to rein you in, and there is no guarantee that they will be kind or convenient. But if you hold fast to the tenet that no matter how much pain you feel this gives you no right to harm the innocent, then you will have protected the body's bottom line and given it the stronger weapon over mind.

12. Those who cannot wholly embrace the energies of the body,

who surrender to the mind's curse upon original self, are doomed to endure conflict and pain. For when one feels lost, it is only original self that is lost. One is only lost in mind. When one goes in search of true self, it is only original self that can be found.

Never could you stand up in the world if another defines who you are and gives you your identity. Others see a superficial "you," only you see your own heart, only you can live out of the center of your being. So why do you continue to live on the surface of their skins? Such a life is not worth a penny. "Vanity of vanities, says the preacher. All is vanity!" Who then is more vain? The master who lives from his heart? Or the servant who lives on the surface of his skin? Or is this the humility that comes from seeing one's self as others see you? Who is the cold-blooded one? Driven from the paradise of his heart, the slave slithers on his belly. The master rules in his heart.

Mastery in the world is not achieved through evil, nor through stupidity. The master can only rule through sanity, in everything. The moral does not demand a different logic from the material. The mind and the body are one. Only slaves divide them. Didn't they themselves say they were given slavery as punishment for their sins? Then if sin gives slavery, goodness alone can give mastery. It is one world and one humanity. What is true for the master, is true for the slave. The master does not live by a different logic. It is the slave who has none.

The truth of the breaking of constraint

13. Here I stand mottled with the blood of the world's most recent slaves. One fraction of myself ranges the world searching for the minutest quantity of blood to lay claim to. At his approach, fearing contamination, all others disown their blood in great haste. In all this running around, where is my center? Where is my philosophy? Rejected by one, denying myself in the other, I must live alone. My own salvation I must find. And I must not fail. Mother and

father I must redeem. Brother and sister I must redeem. Daughter and son I must redeem.

14. In the river of Samsara you could not love as you wanted. You joined others in their mockery of yourself. All that you loved were strewn on the ground. Your heart was torn from you and flung into the darkness. And when it was claimed that the eyes of History had no validity, the child beside the dark river was undermined and could not see through to the burning core—though you stooped and gathered to your bosom the pieces of your broken world. Where is my clear love whose heart I can see, my true love whose center I share? Where is our Aryan womanhood? Where is the manhood of our Aryan childhood? Where is the *ariya loka?* Beneath how many layers of darkness does it lie?

15. If you do not accept the real, then the unreal will draw you in. Understanding is founded on virtue and courage: if you do not accept the truth, then the irrational will place its claim on you and you will lie down with unreason. If you do not accept what you are, all forms are then contorted, truth is an illusion, your eyes are filled with darkness and you do not know the peace of an undivided heart . . .

We were *white* from the day we were born! Why did we invite this blemish upon our hearts? We believed it all. We believed it all. But it was written for slaves; it was written by their masters. While we were renouncers. We were dissenters. How could it ever fit? Whiteness was our *birthright,* but we, of all our brothers and sisters, would not lay claim to it without the license of virtue and courage. We had first to grow in virtue and in courage before we could shun the vile contagion of the dark and right the fallen tree of our mothers and fathers.

16. I have searched everywhere in this blood-smear for the atman which the world has foisted upon me, for that indestructible identity which the world has assured me exists in the blood of their most recent slaves. How could anything exist which, renouncing the world, I could not recover? All were given up in exchange, nothing was ever forthcoming. It is nowhere! It does not exist! If

there is no causal history of a thing, it cannot be produced, though you tear your hair out. How do I share their caste, when harboring their identity I could not love myself? when paying obeisance to their soul was my great hypocrisy? It is a sham! The indestructible atman—then or now—does not exist.

> *"By whom was this kind fashioned?*
> *Where is the one who fashioned it?*
> *From where does a kind rise up?*
> *Where does a kind break up?"*
>
> . . . .
>
> *"A kind! Why do you insist upon this word?*
> *An offensive conceit do you yield to, Mara.*
> *This is its own accumulated causality.*
> *In here no 'kind' can exist.*
>
> *Just as with all the parts united*
> *And the word 'chariot' then assigned,*
> *So it is by propaganda that one speaks of 'kind'*
> *As with the (five) modes existent.*
>
> *It is constraint alone that rises up,*
> *Constraint that settles and withdraws.*
> *Nothing but constraint rises up,*
> *And nothing but constraint breaks up."*[3]

17. So onerous is this badge of honor you award, Mara. So ill-fitting this hand-me-down cloak of darkness. For too long now this sacred cow has given only bitterness. For too long now this illusion has bred only pain and fear. It has irked my mother, irked my father. It has irked brother and sister. But it will not irk daughter and son. Wake up! and shake off Mara's cold hands. Rise up! and give back Mara his hollow names.

18. Betray the brotherhood of Samsara, O Aryan. Eradicate the soul of degradation and squalor, the soul born to such cramped quarters, of condescension and stooped shoulders. No more

walking on eggs! Turn away, give it up, withdraw, make haste from it, *leave!* Renounce the soul and win the world. Destroy it and gain your salvation.

19. In the prison of these eyes, a twin organ misaligned, I sit here and take the heaped up scorn of the world. But a closer prison are these bars and bricks of blood, the which I will so sunder that the other will seem as free as the sky itself. Out of this unbalanced vision, warily do I behold the ones who sought to drown me in my own blood. But I will step from this bloody prison with Dharma eyes, unhappy no more. Let my muse, the noble Anatta, be my witness: I will hone this Dharma voice till it grow to shatter the world, and I stand alone beholding the blackened ruins. This alone is purity, to stand at the end, all else destroyed.

★

20. You were right to be ashamed, my mother, right to be embarrassed, my father. This atman flung against us was fully intended to degrade. It was gathered from out of their foulest midden, mined from their darkest fears, thrown together after their bloodiest carnage and spooked with their most malevolent shades. Let us exorcise this ghost of identity once and for ever: Never! never could we treasure such a heap of oozing sores, such a bloody patchwork! The world's treasures *are* our treasures too.

21. Do you remember, my father, when all the beautiful names were taken, and we were left out owning none? Not to have their names, we thought it was a curse! They thought we were banished forever to that dark, ethnic underground. But we were chosen, my mother, we were chosen. Their names will be the millstone around their necks in the violent waters of Samsara:

> *Those who measure by stigmas and conceits,*
> *They build their refuge in this same way.*
> *Unheedful of the consequences of stigma,*
> *They fall under the rule of death.*[4]

22. Benevolent host! You donate blood to parasites for your own

purity. Your pollution you give to others for their great treasure: a thousand tribes' worth, banished to the underworld, leaving their hearts behind in the world of light, while aboriginals scavenge the slag heap of history and rebuild the lifeless bones to run on a single drop of blood, wizards shrinking entire races upon a red stain, outfitting them for ten thousand years of haunted life on the black river of Samsara.

23. Hypocrites! You hold out *self* denial for others, but for yourselves you choose identity: only others are ethnic, you say, and must deny their selves. But you are the most ethnic of all, fictional travelers who spread their blood abroad but keep its essence at home; lustful destroyers of others' purity but violent defenders of your own. You hypocrites! First pluck out your own demons before you pluck out the demons of others.

Your identity you base on all of your blood, but for the identity of others you allot only an aboriginal fraction. And when you acknowledge all of your heritage it is only right and fitting, but when others acknowledge all of theirs you spread the hurtful lie of their conceit and self-deception. O you contradictory moralists, who sit upon the precipice of blood-identity and push your brothers and sisters over with the yardstick of pollution, O you hypocrites! how many must you send to their agonizing deaths before your bloodlust is satisfied?

24. You accuse the fairer ones of disowning the darker ones, as if there are no gradations among your "own." And I have betrayed my "own," you will say. But black cannot produce white. Only white can produce white. So what of the blood I share with you? Wasn't I disowned? Wasn't I betrayed? What you measure by, and what you distance me with, I have more with you than with them. So where is this uncrossable boundary? Where is this original fault-line? Beneath which unfathomable ocean does this meridian lie? Beyond which impassable sea is this unyielding horizon-line? O Mara, why do you raise again this frightful illusion?

25. These five modes do not fit your color scheme. Yet you continue to insist! Am I supposed to be other than I am? Did some primeval seed take a wrong turn? Does some indissoluble iceberg

lurk in these warm currents? But what you see is just what I am. Thornbushes cannot produce grapes. In the sun there is no ice. Nobility is not made from debasement. Purity is not made from defilement. O Mara, even death is kinder than your kindest word. So let death befall me if I should let you tell me who I am. Let death befall me if I should ever take pride in your silly painted garments. There is no manhood for me in your realm. Bold as you are, you seek to banish me to a meager fraction of my own self. What integrity could I build upon an ethnic quarter, so much less even than the three-fifths fraction you allotted to your slaves? Would that your sons and daughters were confined to such a meager portion of themselves. Where would their honor be then? In what would they take pride? But rather should I be ambushed by death than I should fail to root out your evil seed. A thousand deaths be mine if I should fail to vanquish you and shatter your soul of ice.

26. There is no inalienable stain in my blood. Do not ask how I came by this heritage. It was acquired in the same way that you acquired yours. No outlandish logic governs my inheritance. It is as much mine as anyone else's. It certainly was not stolen. Liars! My parents were not thieves. No way am I alienated from myself. I am the rightful heir of my parents. Eager defamers! You take the testimony of slaves! My father never raped my mother. I am a child of honor. I am a child of honor. I am a child of honor.

27. You reserve nobility for yourselves and deny it to others, as if your sons alone would give their lives to defend the honor of parents. But it is the very honor of my parents that I defend, and upon the truthfulness of their lives that I stand, and from their goodness that I declare that if we could not find our integrity in the world then the world is not fit to survive. For when you flung this slur against us, little did you know how close the world came to being consumed away, so nearly outed was the world's pure light, so nearly overthrown was the world's first innocence. O you, from whose every pore oozes the blackness that envelops the earth, I am not fooled by your whitewashed façade. You are the source

of all the world's darkness, the spot upon the sun, the stain on the lily and the blemish of the fair. You have conspired to defile the sacred core of the universe, you have compelled innocence to defend itself and purity to take up arms. Now feel the wrath. I will fling into the faces of angels and dash into the hearts of saints: there is no precious thing in a world without our integrity. If we are defiled then all the world is defiled. Though you deter me from my manhood and womanhood, I will not be denied. Death be mine, and the world's, if I should fail to win my salvation. So I will fling again this zombie so incredibly hard against your pallid countenance, Mara, that not even ten thousand of your devils working for ten thousand years could put it back together again.

28. O, bhikku, when the golden thread of good intentions has weaved its unbroken pattern, when compassion is all-embracing, when the contradiction of hypocrisy has been eliminated, when you walk doubtless in your virtue, then cast around. You will surely find something which is not constructed, something which is not made, which is not born, something which needs nothing for its sustenance. That is your heart's salvation, for which you have cried throughout the night of your life. And though you leave your virtue, like a soiled shoe, at the door, you will have entered a purity which none may defile, the purity at the center of the universe.

29. Bloodstained is the jeweled world others pretend to. But a world of whiteness and purity is this refuge of Dharma. Here, the devious Mara has been outwitted: I have shattered Mara's indivisible atom and won again the honor of mother and father. His black homunculi I have uprooted: no resentful anger gnaws away my Aryan heart. Pure and white are the seeds of my love. So cloak yourself in the whiteness of virtue, my beloved. No honor can the vile find in this chaste Dharma. Let them keep the virulent red. We will keep the whiteness of Dharma.

30. Bastard sires, you spawn half-begotten alter atmans who hold out identity for others but with their own dishonorable renunciation scamper to the benefits of your own blood-bred

atman; confused souls who marry the daylight yet practice their occult art under cover of darkness; big fishes in little ponds, terrified of open spaces; lukewarm Sonadandas! recognizing the truth of Dharma, but too cowardly to pay homage to the Aryan conquerors of the abysmal ocean.

The self-appointed flag bearers, who in the fight against Mara succumb to a virulent atman and proclaim, in the delirium of their deathbed, a oneness which has never existed except in the hypocritical eyes of sovereign lords and the occult minds of their servile priests; and fall down prostrate before miniature oppressors, parodies of their overlords but still capable of spreading abroad their malicious lies—jealous therewithal of the universals' claim to all the world; and receive extreme unction from homunculus who have no moral hegemony in the world even though they scream at the top of their voices that indeed they do.

31. Shatter the hypocrites' gourd of blood, and like viruses run amok, it will spawn its hologram of alter atmans, its ubiquitous brood existing fully in each alloyed fragment. And ghosts will arise full-blown from every last tithe of blood and scurry back to their black brahmans—worshippers of the blacker Mara—carrying their loot of whiteness to a subject race who profess love of themselves, but truly who love the blood of their oppressors more than they love their own children—so afraid lest they be left alone to the darkness which they themselves invoke; who abhor names from the lips of others, yet demand that the world share their dubious honor and appoint themselves baptizers of other people's children: bloodhounds guarding their master's purity, hiding his indiscretions, exceedingly grateful for the scraps of gore and blood thrown their way; the ferocious slaves, weaned on their masters' blood, they threaten retaliation should anyone deprive them of their elixir, and set about ravishing all the world's bloodlines save their own; black upholders of blackness, but through the alter atman which they so crave with ghosts, black faces which shall have the bluest of eyes.

32. Yet whether they come from the jungles of the Congo or the

puritan heartland of the prairies, whether they come from the Rhineland or the land of Sindh, or even the islands scattered upon the seas, they are all black brahmans, sharing a heart of darkness, carrying in the blood of their eyes a malignant atman, the evil seed that lurks in the mist of their jaundice, the bloodstone smaller than a thumb, that they alone truly *are*. Standing in the shadow that they cast you never emerge from the torpor of an eternal night. Defenders and preservers of the world's dark soul, vain trackers and chroniclers of an illusion who will not let it pass into oblivion, hypocrites feigning blindness yet discerning the one-part-per-million slave blood that is all of a mile away, the merchants of prestige who sabotage all competition for the commodity of whiteness, the perjuring detectives who prove blackness in others from the evidence of their own hearts, and all the smiling dictators proclaiming freedom of speech but employing rule of law reserving for themselves the right to designate your name; know them all, not by their deceiving façades, but for what they rightly are: worshipers of darkness, corrupters and perverters of purity, frantic fighters against the noble Anatta, sepulchering vermin who infect the world's bright spaces with their black plague, demon wizards who conjure darkness in the hearts of innocents.

33. The ravening appetite of the black beast will goad it on, my son. Down every road will stalk the black hound of identity straining at the leash of its sheeted master. Do not let them snare you in their net of categories, my son. Do not let the world tell you who you are. Shadow-hound and ghostly master will carry you away to that grisly river of blood. And there the lurching wash will reach up and draw you in. And you will be lashed for a thousand years on the red violence of that torrent. So hold fast to the pole of your Aryan heritage, my son. Shut the door upon slavering beast and furious master. Fortify the levee of Dharma against the corroding red current. And forever keep watch from the high tower of History.

34. If the laws which protect the most privileged ones cannot protect you, then gladly be charged with treason, gladly be put in

chains, and gladly be sentenced to death. But never accept the begrudged rights of victims, Aryan. Hold to your heart the stark reality of History: *"The deed is, but no doer of the deed is there."*[5] Here lies your liberation and your only court of appeal. Do not seek to invent a "doer" by laying blame. Do not darken the world's light with shades of right and wrong. There is no 'two' in History, there is no 'separate but equal' History. There is only one History. So shun the idolaters and their inferior worship.

35. Do not allow the others to place you on their blacklist of history's injured. A thousand shames on those who dare to make us victims of history. No history oppresses us. We are the fount of History, the scions of History. Here was our courtyard and our playground. We built its high walls and defended from its turrets. Now we are castaways on the wrong side of our battlements and redoubts, while pagan Apollos fling arrow after arrow of poisonous atman to keep us away from our inheritance. Fathers! What have they done to your house? A thousand shames on them for daring to make your sons victims of History.

36. We were *born* in History. Ages ago, on that other isle, we harnessed our speech. And always we have cherished the alphabet upon which we threaded our lives. Yet the mud of envy will bear testimony that our learning is mere mimicry, that our literature is simply rhetoric and our identity pure conceit. Irretrievable atmanists who will not see things as they are, a customary digression of phonemes they read as continental drift and declare a people devoid of literature. And by official proclamation slaves shall avail themselves of your blood—stake their claim in the very hairs of your head, declare you a legitimate son of the fate, and kidnap your heart for Samsara's dark posterity. And the hypocrites will rejoice, proclaiming then their received wisdom, that "what else could a speckled offspring's mother tongue be, but a slave's broken accent?"

37. Scheming siblings, the one you sought to disinherit has come home on the raft of Dharma. Depraved fools, you sullied the innocence of History and dragged it through the muck of your

veins. Blind guides! Blood was the first mire of our fathers. History began when they escaped the great champing wheel of Samsara. That is the first tenet of our Aryan heritage. A thousand shames on you for bloodying the honor of our noble fathers.

38. Primitive moderns, possessed by the ghost of identity, shake off your trance, wake up from your hallucination. Your innermost self, your sacred idol, was hatched on the slag heap, spawned in the crypts and catacombs of Samsara. Spirits of darkness, harbingers of death, you have now been seen! This "fathom-long carcass" no longer will you torment. No fertile soil is found here for Mara's evil seed.

39. Professionals of insecurity, pretenders to whiteness and sophistication, I know the meager little lives you live. Though I have given you my treasures, you could only give me garbage in return: a bridge of deceit was that friendship which hid shame and embarrassment. There is no honor in communion with you. When I did not know you, when I did not know you, how fortunate I was. Now that I have come close, something reeks to high heaven! Renderers of the world's garments, neglectors of the world's unblemished heart, you wagered on the wrong pedigree. Though you were witness to his expert training and were privy to his steadfast discipline, though you bore testimony to the food he fed upon and saw his faultless grooming, yet you turned aside and put your trust in Mara. But the negating son did indeed go to his father's fields. And excellence only looks in the mirror when its hard work is done. I am the one your hearts clamor for. Deaf, dumb and blind: these are the immortally insulting. Long may they live in hell. O Mara, now weep your tears into a river of blood. This Thoroughbred has vanquished the world and won to the golden Nirvana.

40. Do not look upon their atman, my son, compounded as it is out of congealed blood. It will only curdle your own blood and spawn itself in you and you will be driven to that anger which mutilates its owner. That is what they want, that you should sever the arm of your noble heritage. And they will turn away in great

consternation because you refuse to accept the slave identity and the listing through life that they have set for you. Do not satisfy vipers. March, without rancor, into the *ariya loka.* That is your triumph, an ocean traveler's reward. And shut the high doors upon the rabid vampires who daily suck the blood of our Aryan fathers.

41. We are not asking anyone's permission to claim our heritage. We are not offering any apologies for walking away from our pain. The world of History is there for the winning, for those who are willing to make the sacrifice. So never once will we cease to slake the pain inflicted by their arrow of poison with the medicine of the Dharma. A rightful heir does not pretend to his heritage, just as he cannot imitate himself. Jealous householder, soiled by the duties of blood, reality you cannot know. Worthy is the universal born, thus traveled across the churning ocean.

42. It is indeed an insult to associate, and be associated, on the basis of blood. So slay your sacred cow, O Aryan. Do not compromise with ethnic identity. Do not bow to conceit in the one. Do not stoop to join the blood-clubs of the other. Leave these fools in their dance of death. Dealers in blood, all, let us shun. The Eightfold Way is our life line. We have found our way to History. Far be it that you should run now to some dark corner like a beaten dog your tail between your legs.

43. I have made my journey and I have found my peace. The ten thousand cycle captivity is over. Let the world clamor over this discarded raft, seaworthy across the abysmal black whirlpools and the violent white water stretches of Samsara. I have reached the far shore, so let them make use of it or else break it to pieces. There is no more "coming back" for me, already far gone into the heartland.

44. Though no one could have known, through this endless transmigration of identity, that from so far away we were given to the Dharma, to be released upon these stepping stones to the New World, still, let them witness the skillful wielding of the Dharma. Let them witness the healing of every racial hurt. There is no more ambivalence for us. This atman flung against us will wound no

more. The poisonous arrow, the barb in the throat is pulled, the wound has closed. In the Dharma we have found our surety and our purity.

45. Leave others with their blood-bred atman. The Aryan's line of descent is the Eightfold Way. What exquisitely configured aggregate can match the purity of the sublime Nirvana? There is no coming undone here, no breaking apart of ice floes. No pus and bile and phlegm, no parasite carrying blood clog this realm; no sagging, wrinkled and blotched membranes hang within here; no wheezing, no choking fit of coughing, no sagging strength quiver this realm. So leave fools to take their ghost ride through the generations; leave fools to seek a perverted pleasure in birth repeated again and again and fall to blows again and again. There is no more coming back to be of blood, flesh and bones in the Aryan way.

Unfounded, O monks, is the ancestry of this Samsara. A prototype is not demonstrated for (those) kinds which, molded in ignorance and enslaved to compulsion, are scurrying and scrambling upon this haunting of the generations.[6]

The truth of the way that leads to the breaking of constraint

46. I will never agree to being cast out of philosophy and dispossessed of the world. I will not allow honor to be shared out among men and I receive none. I will not accept for myself and bequeath to my children a slave's identity. It is a coward who answers when another is called. It is a fool who submits to the taunting of history and society. I will not lay my honor, or my children's honor, upon another's reputation. I will not live my life a slur upon the world's tongue. I will not be placed on society's injured list. No history oppresses me. Why, History is my liberation. A slave to History is a freeman, if they but know. Be thankful for your enslavement to History, for therein lies your liberation. Those whom History

balked at enslaving for so long, aren't they the most depressed? Those whom the mill of History did not tread underfoot in ancient times, aren't they the ones filled with shame and humiliation? Aren't they the ones who hate themselves?

47. Their identity is a sore in other men's eyes, but your own burning cancer. Their Africa was founded long before Vasco da Gama sailed along its coasts, long before Columbus set sail for the New World. This heart of darkness exists in the primeval past of everyman. Why do you alone wear it as a badge of honor? It is everyman's sores and hurts, everyman's fears. Why do you alone cry? It is everyman's neuroses, everyman's schizophrenia. Why are you alone driven mad? This identity is the dumping ground of the world, all the world's slag heap. It is everyman's filth and mud, everyman's dirt. Why are you alone soiled? In everyman's enslavement, everyman's humiliation, why do you alone serve? Why are you alone fickle? The boils and sores of the world you treasure. The world's cankers are your shrine. You polish everyman's scab and scream in ecstatic pain at everyman's hurt. Honorary brahman! not owning property, practicing self-torture and claiming moral superiority through suffering: hypocrite loving purity but only in its pollution: harboring the world's indestructible stain, staining all, unwashed by any: you joined their ranks not as eager proselyte, but as pollution and refuse! Aryan! Why do you alone enshrine darkness? Why do you alone seek light without a flame? Light gathers light and darkness breeds darkness. You alone multiply your darkness and cry in vain for light. How much longer will you continue to balance upon a sliver of tainted blood?

48. Ethiopia! Ethiopia! When your blameless mother was taken, why did you abandon the care of your younger siblings? Self-satisfied older one that you are, you left them to wander about unclothed and unschooled. Still they turn their eyes to you in awe. Ethiopia! Ethiopia! You could not carry the torch of civilization but for yourself. Your brothers stumbled beside you in the dark.

Why then should I praise you, Ethiopia? Other royal houses have held court for much shorter periods than you and yet have

116

transformed great expanses and subcontinents. Didn't you believe as they did? Deserts elsewhere have known the light of civilization, and the deepest forests. Were you afraid to venture forth? But as an older sibling who failed his mother's promise you deserve to be scolded, scoffed at and rebuked. For when the danger ravished your mother's own, where were you? You with the eyes to see, you failed to see. With staff to guide you failed to show the way. A continent's reward you turned your back upon.

Your unmindfulness has proven you a sluggard, unworthy of the accolades and awe that your ill-bred siblings are wont to lavish on you, all your mythmakers with paper and pen, your concrete thinkers, your crude rationals—primitive moderns who flounder in the backwaters of civilization and history. Shamans, all, who conjure the dead, while all around them the living swarm. How they treasure your dark relics and turn from the light. Staring backwards at you they stumble into the future.

49. If your notions of selfhood are grounded in the irrationality of a preknowledge, you open a wide door to impulsiveness and fear. You surrender control to sentimentality and randomness. You withdraw the light of reason; you sever the artery of life and cradle stillborn little lives. So along the highway of your blind allegiance will hasten from every direction the darkness of unreason and chaos like barbs to your hearts. And everywhere you congregate, your societies flounder in impotence. You writhe in agony, you cower in fear and lash out in anger, but nothing will avail you. For you yourselves have enthroned unreason and given a home to darkness.

50. I will not defend racial identity for the sake of others. I will not stand on the backs of fools, drowning as they are in the murky waters of self-delusion, so that I alone may gasp the clean air of the open surface. Where is my love if I should gather the treasures of the wide world but require others to search only a dark corner? Where is my honor if I should choose the manhood of History for myself but recommend the identity of the primitive for others? There is no self-harmony here, there is no union of mind and body

here, there is no peace here. There is only conflict and disharmony, and the heart's painful severance, the tearing at the hair and the wasting of the flesh. There is only *dukkha* here.

51. Mara's priests will protest that their atman is reality, fact: it is no metaphysical creation: it is there for everyone to see: it is in their complexion, the configurations of their bones, the texture of their hair: it is their fathers' gift to them, their exclusive inheritance. Where was this identity, though, before its opposite? It was in the helical DNA molecule, where it belongs. It is only the racial identity which remains in this molecule that is not a metaphysical creation. All else is superstition. That identity which they wear so proudly as a badge of honor, I certainly did not inherit through the DNA molecule, but through its superficial opposite, through the incredulity and amazement of others, through their ridicule, their insecurity and immorality. This is my inheritance, the mockery of another, this is my highest ideal which they recommend, this is my deepest self, the ridiculous laughter, the buffoonery of another. This is the vile incongruity which I must inculcate in my heart. Must they still wonder why I am so irretrievably estranged from that vile conjurer's trick, from that dark feat of wizardry, that summoning of malevolent spirits, mirage of hair, skin and bones, which is their professed honor? But such a surface identity, such a superficiality, such a dark, foreboding self I abjure, I reject unconditionally. Their counter culture, their underground culture, their culture of reaction I will have none of. Their ethnic identity I spurn.

[T]he body is alien to you, reject it. Rejecting it will be to your benefit, to your well-being. Expression is alien to you . . . Impression is alien to you . . . the configurations are alien to you . . . entrancement is alien to you, reject it. Rejecting it will be to your benefit, to your well-being.[7]

52. How unwholesome is this atman, how unpleasant this occult buddha, how utterly *other* is this bloodied soul. Like a hook in your throat, like gravel in your eye, like a parasite moling your

flesh is this identity, its eye, its ear, its nose, its tongue, its body and its mind. Too confounding is this hideous conceit of hair, skin and bones! There is *nothing* persisting anywhere in it despite what Mara and his black priests say.

Body, expression, impression, configurations and entrancement are impermanent. And that which is impermanent is afflicted with constraint. And that which is afflicted with constraint (that is, impermanence) is without transgenerational identity. And of that which is not one's self, one should acknowledge in accordance with reality and with full consciousness: 'This is not my own, I am not this, this is not my Identity.'[8]

So discerning, the well-schooled Aryan Disciple admits aversion for the body, for expression, for impression, for configurations, for entrancement. Admitting aversion he extricates himself, being extricated he is freed, and in freedom is the knowledge of being freed and he comes to know: 'Cut off is rebirth, practiced is the moral life, accomplished is all that needed to be accomplished, there is no future production (willed) for this form.'[9]

53. I have left the multitudes behind in the streets and squares going about their metaphysical penance. I have seen my truth and make haste to my Nirvana, this History, this Aryan heritage. The bloodthirsty idol of the priests I have toppled! The dark spell is broken. No more for me the great churning ocean and the ignorance of my true nature. No more for me the denouncing of light. The dark world is renounced. Today I have become a kinsman of the **adicca.** How great is my joy! How my lungs gulp this new element I now see was mine before anything else. How my bosom expands and my muscles flex and my limbs acquire great strength and freedom.

54. The ghost of no ancestor will I harbor. *"Rooted out [is] all life's continuance."*[10] These five modes will be no way station for evil spirits hellbent into the future. No spirit will thread me upon Samsara's necklace of death. No black priest will thumb me in his

samsaric rosary. Your string of blood is broken, demons, and forever will stay. Dance in agony around your broken circle. Never will it join again in me. No ring of blood will I dance. No savage ritual will I practice. You could even call upon your ghostly master, Mara, the giver of blood-names, never will your circle be tied again in me. So coffle your own selves, you pack of demons driven on by Mara. March in exact rhythm through the wilderness of Samsara, and go to your eternal hold upon the whipping ocean. This one has loosed all bonds and never more will pay allegiance to master and slave. Never more will he be held and whipped upon ocean by condescension and by Mara's vile name-calling.

55. Their crying drove you to your knees in that conceited "worship of the word "we.""[11] Your deluded guilt stooped your shoulders and broke your resolve. Your pity smeared your face all over with the world's filth. In your heart's great anathema you sought redemption: you martyred yourself to degradation and squalor and crowned yourself king of the unaryan. Lotus blossom! Heed your true nature! The swirling distress could never have reached your heart. Else you would long ago have been broken upon the granite rocks of this black river. Rescued Aryan! Do not leave these high grounds again. Do not forsake your unsoiled heart for the dirty garments of the world.

56. Thus traveled, O sacred self, do not give a lodging to the dark rider of the night. He will only ingratiate himself for the lifetime, and at the sad end discard the carcass, thankless, upon the slag heap of Samsara for another. More skillful than any pimp, more times than a thousand men go through garments, he goes through bodies, making his way down the generations, his sole desire to taste again and again the bitterness of death. One should halt this ghostly rider in his mad rush, cut him off in his deadly stampede. Do not make of yourself a doorway to his bitter future. He can only ride upon your five modes as steed. Do not give free passage to this serial killer of the world.

57. Long have I searched for that logic which would lock our hearts into reason. Never again to be dismayed, the logic of

Dharma I have found. And I declare: In the Aryan there is no moral defect. We could never stand up in the world if we left our hearts unresolved. Hypocrites we never were, never once did we betray our love. Just as they received their rebounding heart, so we received our unimpeded heart. True love has never needed the foul canal of blood. Why should it be required of our love? Why should our love alone be confined to the underground pathways of Samsara?

But I have mastered the Dharma's logic and with it I here cast off the world's vile imposition. To that flawed syllogism which says, "You love, therefore you are," I respond, "Identity is never the perfection of love; it is rather in the extrication from blood that love is perfected." So do not deceive yourselves. My love of the world is not an exotic love. It is the same love that you have for your mothers and fathers, for your brothers and sisters, your daughters and sons. There is no alien germ in my heart. I am the wide world. *DEVILS INCARNATE ARE THOSE WHO DECREED THAT MY LOVE SHOULD FOUNDER IN THE MIRE OF BLOOD.*

Compassion does not come from identity, and it is impossible that compassion could produce such an illusion. Identity was never the goal of love, but that unconditional sundering of the dark, the sublime Nirvana which severs every bond, that is the only fitting goal for your love. That truly is the reward of compassion; rejoice, and do not be dismayed. To assert "I am" is not thereby to love. The nature of compassion is to alleviate pain, not to find pleasure in it: it is because your love was true that you never could say "I am" to tainted blood. Rest your mind. There is nothing suspect in a love without identity. You have been true: rest your mind. To that which the world says, "You are," respond, "I am not." And to that which the world says, "You are not," respond, "I am." That is to create balance and equanimity. Only the envious will not allow this classical logic of our classical condition.

58. From ancestral homes in the far north we traveled in our frail caravels to islands scattered on the warm seas. Upon this long way we fell out among ourselves and in the deep hold beneath

enslaved the dark portion of our souls. And there we have remained for hundreds of years besieged on either side by our hearts' bitterness. But through this long transmigration of identity how was this European ever tainted except in his joy? How was this Caucasian ever polluted except through suffering? Abolish the status of one fraction of yourself as a pollutant, Aryan! Abolish the status of one fraction of yourself as a stain, undiluted even when immersed in another ten thousand times its own weight. And wander through the world settling everywhere, being a part of every family, no longer an outcast. My Aryan heart, my Aryan heart, I have come home to you! To purge mother and father of tainted blood, to purge brother and sister, daughter and son, I have brooked the eternal Mara. My Aryan eyes, my Aryan eyes, I have reclaimed you! I have slain the foul Mara who had sought to blacken thee.

A declaration

59. Everywhere one turns in this land there stand the children of slaves, bondsmen still clamoring for the rights of freedmen one hundred years into their emancipation, carried in tour to every corner of this land by masters who, even if their lives depended on it, could not conceive of honor without servants underfoot. This is no **ariya loka!** This is slave country. Everywhere there are reminders to the victimization of their locals. Yet still not satisfied they cultivate the fantasy of universal oppression. Collectors of medals to conceit and vanity, they gather from around the world the children of noble heritage only to subject them to a phantom oppression of the past. Their citizens' hard-filled treasury they squander in reparations to imaginary victims. Across the land they drag their chain of blood and shackle Aryans with slaves. The pompous pedagogues! to Aryans they dare condescend to teach the ABCs of civilization. And yet, the language expropriators that they are, they deny to English men and women the full license of

English: rationing out names, they give curses to others and keep honorifics alone for themselves. You are getting old, you brood of Mara, and slipping, even in this your last refuge: these fantastic feats of oppression are the sure signs of senility. You have never enslaved me, or my mother and father, or even their mothers and fathers—but only in your atman of so vile conceit. Slave souls perpetuate only in slaves. And well you know that one man could not enslave himself. We have never betrayed that beauty carved by the sword of victory. We have never been broken by the ugliness molded in slavery and defeat.

60. Where did you get that garage-sale atman from, my boy, that you treasure so in your heart? Did Mara clean out his attic today? Nay. Did he clean out his basement—his sodden, dank and musty basement? Did he sell it to you for a dime? For a penny? Or did he give it to you, as it were, in charity, no other customer obliging? Did he glue it together from the broken pieces of his children's dolls? Did he throw in the chewed-off ends of his daughter's toy menagerie, the hackneyed limbs from his princely son's toy farm? Did he supply you with those smelly rags? If so, then there is a bridge I would most gladly sell you . . . O, but pardon me, sir. Since Mara in his great impudence has seen fit to forcibly impregnate me with this rag doll, then I reserve the right to besmear it and besmirch it and dash it into the mud and slime of the vilest gutter! Go retrieve your rag doll, boy, from the gutter where it lies. Go call in your warrantee, and the warrantor to remedy my disdain.

61. No devil will scare me out of myself to look with alien eyes upon my very own heart. No besieged master will make of me an olive branch to his revolting slaves. I am not the ransom for my tormentor's freedom. Neither am I the illegitimate spawn of some shameless autocrat, to be disowned in his public policy. I am not a commodity to be passed from oppressor to oppressed with built-in obsolescence to become the worthless property of slaves. I am my own self. In this bitter war I do not take advice from my enemy on whom my allies should be, on where I should dig my trenches, build my fortifications and what weapons I should

employ: Mara has never been the self-immolating kind who would guide his adversary to victory. There are different loyalties here. Their honor is not my honor. Their allegiance is not my allegiance. We uphold different truths. We give our lives for different ends. In its swaggering arrogance the world has sought my injury, the dishonor of my mother and father, and the hurt of those I love and of those who love me; has sought my eternal humiliation and shame. Yet I have not been harsh enough. I should have destroyed the world rather than admonish it.

62. I do not seek to be what I am not. I merely defend myself from destruction: I reject an alien manhood for the child of my mother and father. To submit to the identity of someone else's construing is to die to one's own self. And when a man dies to himself, he is no more than a beast. There is no life for men without integrity, and the first integrity is the acceptance of one's true nature. What greater oppression is there than the usurpation of one's heart? What nobler endeavor is there than the repelling of the thorns against one's heart? It is for the heart's release that the father goes to war, though to remain at home would revoke the usurper's threats upon the welfare of his family. It is for the unbroken nurturing of the heart that the father will discipline his son in the art of war. There is no life but this life, its honor and disgrace; no death like the death to one's own self. There is no freedom greater than the freedom of the heart.

63. I, an Aryan, knowing I am an Aryan, without taints, should come now to this place and be set upon by such eager slanderers! Yet what is this but a clash of values, a clash of cultures. Sheltering for twenty-nine years in the home of my mother and father, I always knew myself. I never went into their neighborhoods, was never insulted, never came into their company, and never saw the works of Mara's hands till I could defend my heart against all the world. What is wrong with these who do not know me or anything about me or where I am from, but would tell me who I am and what my heritage should be? who would burden me with an alien lineage? who would conscript me as their enemy? What manner of

hosts are these? Is this how a stranger is treated in their land, the innocent lured into the dark pit of their foul contrivance? Who are they who would imprison me in my own self? Who are they but Mara in disguise. Who are they who would break in upon my sanctuary and banish me against my will to the darkest corridors of my being? Who are they but Mara in disguise. Who are they who would throw thorns in my way? Who are they but Mara in disguise. Who are they who would deny me my manhood? Who are they but Mara in disguise. I told you who I was. But you would not believe me. So I had no choice but to disrobe you before the eyes of History. And grotesque as you are I will not run away in fear. I will not be quartered by earth's great murderer, and flung upon his reeking midden. I will not commit suicide. I will not commit patricide. I will not commit matricide. I will succor all my family.

64. Planters of Dharma upon English soil, we have toiled in this work for generations. But even in that which I dominate I have no respect. Every fool seems so eager to instruct me in the error of my ways. It must be the plank in their eyes which makes them to see configurations of the five modes where there are none. But I must accept: what is honor for some, is my own eternal humiliation. For myself, the alternative to white is not black. It is cowardice. Despite what they say, though, I do not identify with others. I identify with myself. It is vanity to seek to be like others. My whiteness never belonged to anyone else. It always existed in me. So in vain do the envious seek to usurp my heart.

65. It has taken this long to accept what they have been gawking at all my life: I have been born for the perfection of Dharma. It is in the purity of the childhood which would register such profound shock and incredulity at the reception of the barbarians, who in malicious envy sought to strangle the manhood of this childhood. Where did they think I came from: the underside of the world? Who did they think I was? O, my mother and father, do they think they know better than you what child you brought into the world? And do they think I would give my allegiance away from love and

its pronouncements to the slurs of hatred and insecurity? Truly have they miscalculated. They must have thought I would be daunted by that which they are daunted, cowed by that which they are cowed, and awed by that which awes them, *that they would seek to put me in my place!* Did they think I was homeless, without a mother and father, without a heritage, that they would force-feed this bit of foul-smelling meat, this clot of blood, when they know full well it is poison for the heart? And to demand the payment of gratitude! O, the conceit, the conceit and arrogance! Raze! raze! the temple of impudence to the ground, break its pillars and shatter its walls, scatter its cups and bowls, and spill its unholy liquids into the gutter, tear at its dark scrolls and drag, drag its vestments through the defiling, ruinous mud!

66. It is indeed given to each to wield what he will. And as it is given to the offensive ones to wield a bureaucracy and a social system, so it is given to me to wield the Dharma. I have been born for the sole purpose of founding Dharma upon these shores. And it is I who will say who is worthy to be saved and who must be damned. And damned, I say, are the offensive ones who stain purity, who wallow in blood and require others to wallow in blood, who cast aspersions upon and slur the noble Anatta, who in their public places rape the innocent and strip the manly of their manhood, damned are they and their applauding courts. Damned again are those who seek to defile a Tathagata. They would assign you a slave's quarters, and yet would expect to be given this Dharma as tribute, as a captive would to his conquering masters. Nay. But they incur a wrath which they could not endure. They are driven from the refuge of Dharma to make their homes forever in the confines of hell. They are staked for an eternity upon the burning wheel of Samsara. They shall not find salvation in this Dharma or any other Dharma. Let them flounder helplessly in their rag-doll yoga. Their alibi of convention will not avail them. Not even ten thousand saints pleading on their behalf could save them from their damnation. They are damned for an eternity. They are damned for an eternity. They are damned for an eternity's eternity.

67. If I had known them in my tenderness, then would the world have hated itself, then would first principles have been corrupted and assuredly the universe have self-destructed. But when a world is created its devils are never plucked from the crystalline heavens. When a world is created its devils are molded from dirt and soil and all things base. Impossible that I would permit these vilest of creatures to dictate to me the dimensions of my life. Impossible that I would permit these witches and warlocks to barb my hair, to char my complexion and dehumanize my form. And most impossible of all, that I would permit these shameless corrupters to make a vice of my virtue. *Alone* is my integrity the support of this world. I make the world. And I destroy it. So let them be aware: When I made the world I made Aryans pure. I made devils to taunt and slur, and live in vain.

68. You *must* allow the hypocrites to go their sullen ways. You look them in the faces only at your great distress. For there, in its position of honor, resides the dark atman—that abomination for which they have labored all of their deceitful lives—ever vigilant as it rides upon the iris of their prestige-mongering eyes. They will say, "Our Supreme Court has not ruled on it." But why do they think I await their grudging decision—vain words on vain paper? Rather I submit myself to the verdict of History—certain and irreversible. So though they tender their excuses, this is no priest selling indulgences. All has been accomplished: they sought my injury; and I defended myself. The names may not ever again be recalled. And History cannot be rewritten.

69. Again and again do the generations come, wave upon exuberant wave, yet all foundering upon the shores of mortality. But when the heaving sea has brought its teeming load, only the buddhas will know these shores as haven against the drowning ocean. Securing one's heart in this, yet giving a home to usurpers would indeed be vain. So today, when the heart is firm, are the disinheritors disinherited. They were the ones wont to avert their eyes and disavow you before their kind, as if their fount of blood held more prestige than the sublime Nirvana. But I shall disown

them before the noble Anatta, refuse to acknowledge them in the neighborhoods of Dharma. So who are the losers now? By which other path shall they attain release? A plague upon the earth, indeed, are the atmanists. Into their black hearts they suck the brightness of the sun. Arise, Anatta soldier, and banish them from the reality they love so much to deny. They are foundered, one another, in the bitter waters of illusion.

70. Come, my son, let us sing the defeat of Mara. In this long journey through Samsara all the myriad cunning forms of the Deceiver have I encountered. "Tailor of illusions! you told the world I was clothed in darkness, and all the world turned away, everyone was ashamed of me, no one would be seen in my presence. What an ass to be to sit and be measured for Mara's suit of shame! But I am naked, I am naked, as to the day I was born, let the world perceive! Crude sculptor! who distorted my eyes, my ears, my nose, my lips, and painted so grotesquely my complexion, your ludicrous clown I have sorely angered, your stiff-necked puppet I have broken, your fearsome scarecrow I have torn to pieces, for this frog-prince his princess has seen. Fraudulent scientist! where is that virulent germ you claim to have discovered swimming in my blood? Where is that everlasting homunculi, prized heirloom of my family? Where are its eyes, its ears, its nose and lips, its arms and legs, its black torso? What a hoax you have perpetuated upon the world, given the long lie even to the blood." Come sing the release from the bonds of Samsara, my son. An ass do not be for Mara's morbid attire.

71. Beware of the apprentices who, cast as monkeys with the flesh of the swine that is so abhorrent to them, have inherited their masters' mold. Of their own transition to human status they have made a hypocrisy: they would love nothing better than that their reprehensible behavior be branded with the distinction of blood. But it is the same old immorality which abuses the mother and father, which rapes the sister and murders the brother, which fights down the cousin. Isn't it ironic that they who were held at arms length in the Old World, should in the New, in just two genera-

tions, drive others away? who, then, desperate to escape the stain of blood, should now so zealously inflict it on others? Pariahs in the ancestral home, hounded to near extinction, in the colonies their blood salvation they have found: they have inducted themselves into the fold, foot soldiers frantically defending the base degrees of whiteness.

72. In Mara's school of yoga, you can only attain to his atman if you are a coward, only if you are a broken man, a defeated man, only if you pander to the provincial born of the world. And while you are learning his dark scriptures he will steal the wealth of your heart. And you will become a stranger to yourself, a haunted shadow of your father's child. Others will learn your language and mock your own accent. They will take offence at your lingering love of home and self. And you will be driven from the heartland where you were born, where your father was born, where his fathers before him were born. Roadblocks will be placed along the bloodstreams of your inheritance, and strangers, from the ends of the earth, will claim right of passage, while you are turned back. And every morning, just for the privilege of being a transit servant in your own house, you will be stripped and searched. And what in your heart they can never find, they will yet stitch upon your sleeve and stamp upon your forehead. An alien culture will be given to sprout upon your heart. You will be chattel in your own land. And happily you will feed upon your very self. Profaned are all your sacred places, then, and ravished the land that held your dreams. Till you come to know how it feels to live without a heart, to be like wood and stones, to have eyes and still not see, ears and still not hear, a tongue that cannot taste, arms that hold no love. —Let the universal born know himself. He is the fullest creation. Let him not defer to the provincial born of the world. Truly must these be brought under the Dharma that they may lose their insularity and admit the world.

73. All the universal born are sons and daughters of the Dharma. For where else may their integrity be found? Where else is their security, and their defense against the world? In which other

Dharma are their manhood and womanhood assured? In which other Dharma is the unbroken nurturing of their children? There is no Dharma like a Dharma that looks to your happiness and welfare. So what will bend the uncouth and ill-bred to show their due respect? What will lift up the universals' honor in the world? And what will foil the violent attacks of the marauding hordes? Didn't the noble Anatta redeem the universal born? Didn't it clear the way to the great sundering? Every name I took became tainted on Mara's vile tongue. So I sought the one place where names have no basis. And now I call home, from the ends of the earth, all the prodigal Aryans to the mansion of the Dharma.

74. It seems like only yesterday when we were driven out of the fold. Against our will the values we shared with them were stripped of their proper name. Universal born, we were deemed polluted. Their salvation we could no longer share. But little did they know that by choosing, they had forfeited their own salvation. And so we wandered off, each alone, into the wilderness of Samsara. And there through cold and darkness, through so many cycles of pain and fatal arrows have we sought our own salvation. And it is a good salvation that we have found. As it was said so very long ago, it still is so today:

It is because we did not understand, did not penetrate the four Aryan truths, O monks, that I as well as you have trekked for so long upon this haunting of the generations. Now what are these four truths? They are the Aryan truth of Constraint, the Aryan truth of the Cause of Constraint, the Aryan truth of the Breaking of Constraint, and the Aryan truth of the Way that leads to the Breaking of Constraint.[12]

★

75. How is the commodity of whiteness produced? For what currency is it exchanged? And how is it consumed? By adversity is it produced, for humility is it exchanged, and in jealous rivalry

130

is it consumed. See how the fools of the world barter and sell themselves in pursuit of this illusion. But never will Mara get his white-hot boost from me. There is no tar in my blood, no obscurity in me whereby Mara's death mask could be alchemized to the fool's gold of whiteness. The purity of the Aryan is undisputed: he does not treasure taints and cankers. I am an Aryan because no blood pollutes me. I am an Aryan because no blood of mine is tainted. I am my original self; I am the child my mother and father made; I have not fallen; I have not been corrupted, neither my mother nor my father. We have been purebred for thousands of generations. From time immemorial have we been trueborn, sons and daughters of the one world. What a lie do they tell otherwise. All the world's diversity are made one in us. So even you who throw your children away, yet return upon them again and again to rape their innocence with your foul insults, even you I hold out compassion to.

76. Turn away from the scornful ones who say, "Look! They have embraced those who insulted them." Where else is the best proving ground for our hearts but this front of the world? And in meeting the challenge of these, haven't we garnered this most excellent Dharma and proved ourselves worthy of all the world's heritage? My son and daughter, you must dominate the Dharmas of the world, master the world's disciplines and always place yourselves at their centers. Make the world after your own image and the image of those who love you and see themselves as one with you. Let your ears be the best, let your eyes be the best, let your nose and lips be the best, let your countenance be the best. But do not let them make you their enemy. Do not grant them their death wish. Don't they know that if we were other than them, that if we were indeed what they say we were, then we would be filled with bitterness? And do they think that in revenge we would bungle the destruction of the world? But do not let them make you their enemy. Treasure the world and those of them that love you and strive to place yourselves at the summit.

77. It is only in the fullest practice of the Dharma that all taboos

are broken and all boundaries traversed. What is life for but to seek fulfillment? I have sought my fulfillment and I have found it. Let the naysayers cast their remarks. Truly is the Dharma a revolutionary discipline. Not possible is it that the Dharma could be handled and the handler should shrink away. If in the practice of Dharma the world must be destroyed, then the world will be destroyed. No toy Dharmas for us. We will have the real thing, that cuts like a knife and bleeds like a river the improper handler. So gather up the firewood of virtue, my son, and set fire to the stains and cankers of blood. There are no heights unreachable by Dharma.

78. A blood-bred atman is the fiction that rules the world of men. But this identity supports no knowledge, it gives no understanding, it heals no wound. It is in fact the first wound, the first ignorance, the eternal darkness. It is the bane of understanding, and the enemy of Dharma, the high fence in the way of Nirvana. There is no liberation with this identity. So one must find it out, and root it out where it lies in the heart, your precious atman, and dash it against the diamond rocks of the Dharma and walk away to your salvation.

79. I am proud to say I live from the heart. The world does not outweigh me. I outweigh the world. This blood is not heavier than that blood. Not possible is it, I say, that a synthetic atman concocted in the workshops of Mara could outweigh the timeless Aryan heart.

It is the noble Anatta which men have worshipped from time immemorial, in which they have placed their hopes and faith, for which they have gone to war and taken respite, for which the cities have been built and for which they have been destroyed. And for this again will the swords flash and the rivers run crimson. For this again will the world know turmoil and know peace. To that which has saved my life, I pledge my life. To that which has given me my life, I give back my life and the lives of my children. I will proclaim my salvation to all. I will establish it upon the earth and defend it against all the world.

The Tathagata stands in the perfection of the noble Anatta, the bright void where Mara, Prince of Darkness, may not enter. He bears no marks of Mara's great impudence, no incongruous appendages of Mara's rag doll: no eyes—though he sees, no ears—though he hears, no hands—but he holds, no feet—but he walks. Unseen, unheard, unfelt, unreached, the Ineffable: this is the Aryan heart, the bright well of the universe.

80. The world of identity is not a world of color. It is a bleak world in black and white. It is a pale, sunless place, a shadowy stage of flitting shades, a ghost realm. Only the nonexisting of identity bestows reality. Turn on the light of Anatta and observe how the shadows vanish and the real is defined. It is only this nonexisting which gives happiness its flavor, which gives beauty its color. There is nothing above the noble Anatta. It stands supreme through all the ages.

81. There is so much nonexistence in the world. So many things do not exist. This jewel! This ocean of light, this brightness stretching forever. There is no crag here, no corner, no dark place. There is no dust, no dirt. This is not death! This is the end of illusion. This brightness which does not need the sun, nor the moon. It brims with clarity, it brims with sanity! Why does the world spurn this treasure? It is everywhere, all around. So many things do not exist. There is so much nonexistence in the world.

82. Life is a succession of moments and opportunities; while death is one single moment, that shutting off of all possibilities. But anxiety makes of death an infinity of moments and of life a living hell. It is ever the atman, cloaked in the illusion of idealism and perfectionism, which breeds distress; which yet seeks the unconditioned within the five modes. It would have you stumble and hurt yourself, all because it could not accept the necessary arrangement of reality; it would have you cut yourself and bruise yourself in its compulsion to override the causal necessity of reality. But just as you do not hurt yourself against the contours of space, so must you not hurt yourself against these contours of mind. Allot to death its one meager moment while you awaken to

the fullness of life. Death occurs at the end of life, never in the middle, and never in the beginning.

83. I think of my parents' longings, and their desires for me in that bright morning of the child, the storehouse of my values, and now I think to myself: This is the world my parents pointed out to me as a child; this is the world I was brought up to inherit. This is the manhood and womanhood of my childhood! This is the final homecoming! I have searched vainly for half my life through the labyrinth of the aboriginal wilderness. Right here before me, rising out of the clinging mud, I see the rock-hewn steps of the Dharma! What joy to have finally arrived in that Aryan household, and walk with my fathers who made a great adventure of the wide world, in this History, this top of the world which is everything, beyond which there is nothing. Here there is no constraint. Here I rule my fate.

84. There is nothing above History, and nothing beyond. It is our finest flowering, our final home, our whole salvation, the bright sky where the gods walk. The buddhas do not escape History. They are History's greatest achievement. It is only they who truly know and embody History. They have always been its last and fiercest defenders. They appear when civilization is in the throes of decay, seek out its moral roots, its rational basis, and preserve its essence throughout the devastation of ruin, not in civilization's works of art or products of commerce, but in themselves, their consciousness, their awareness. And carry it safely beyond sloth and stagnation to fertile soil and long fallowed fields.

Notes to essays

ESSAY I

1. This estrangement is most certainly a reflection of the physical barrier of the Sahara desert itself, a barrier as formidable as the Himalayas and steppes of central Asia. These geographical boundaries, though straddling continuous land masses, were (and are) as alienating as oceanic bodies of water. On opposing sides different cultures and even races have been able to develop independently. The Mediterranean, as a barrier, pales in significance compared to the Sahara, so that Egypt had much more of an impact upon the Mediterranean world, of Europe and Asia, than upon sub-Saharan Africa, and in turn was impacted by Europe and Asia much more than by the world of Africa south of the Sahara.

2. Amy Jacques Garvey, ed. *The Philosophy and Opinions of Marcus Garvey* (New York: Atheneum, 1980).

3. Bonnie K. Holcomb and Sisai Ibssa, *The Invention of Ethiopia* (Trenton, NJ: Red Sea Press, 1990).

4. Derek Walcott was awarded the noble prize for literature in 1992. He teaches at Boston College in the U. S. A.

5. V. S. Naipaul, "A Plea for Rationality," *Indians in the Caribbean,* ed. I. J. Bahadur Singh (New Delhi: Sterling, 1987), 17–30.

6. Michael Carithers, *The Buddha,* Past Masters (Oxford and New York: Oxford Univ. Press, 1983), 20.

7. V. S. Naipaul, *Finding the Center* (London: André Deutsch, 1984; reprint, Harmondsworth: Penguin Books, 1985), 38.

8. V. S. Naipaul, *The Mimic Men* (London: André Deutsch, 1967; reprint, Harmondsworth: Penguin Books, 1969), 151.

9. V. S. Naipaul, *Guerrillas* (New York: Alfred A. Knopf, 1975; reprint, New York: Vintage International, 1990), 32–34.

10. *ibid.,* 57.

ESSAY I

11. V. S. Naipaul, interview by Ian Hamilton, "Without a Place," *Times Literary Supplement* (30 July 1971): 897, quoted in John Thieme, *A Critical View on V. S. Naipaul's "The Mimic Men"* (London: Collins, 1985), 27–28.

12. Though Naipaul is a perennial candidate for the Noble Committee's literary prize, he has not won it so far. He does not, however, lack for prestigious literary awards, and in 1990 was awarded a knighthood by the British. But the noble prize will never be a true estimate of the talent and significance of either Naipaul or Walcott.

13. V. S. Naipaul, *A Bend in the River* (New York: Alfred A. Knopf, 1979; reprint, New York: Vintage International, 1989), 3.

14. *ibid.,* 20.

15. *ibid.,* 244.

16. *ibid.,* 151–152.

17. John Keats, "Ode to a Grecian Urn," *Collins Albatross Book of Verse* (London: Collins, 1960), 375.

18. Naipaul, *The Mimic Men,* 56–57.

ESSAY II

1. A clear statement of the social reality of ancient India can be found in Kogen Mizuno's *The Beginnings of Buddhism,* trans. Richard L. Gage (Tokyo: Kosei Publishing, 1980), 3–5.

2. The modern expression of this Upanishadic philosophy was given by the Russian-born American writer, Ayn Rand (1905–1982). In her writings Ayn Rand employed the 'self' or atman idiom of the *Upanishads* in its original, rational meaning. For a concise and very passionate introduction see Ayn Rand, *Anthem* (London: The Caxton Printers, *n.d.*; reprint, Harmondsworth: Penguin, Signet, *n.d.*).

3. I. Schloegel, *The Zen Teachings of Rinzai* (Boulder: Shambala Publications, 1976), 43, quoted in Judith Blackstone & Zoran Josipovic, illustrated by Naomi Rosenblatt, *Zen for Beginners* (London: Writers and Readers Documentary Comic Books & Unwin Paperbacks, 1986), 92.

ESSAY II

4. The Dhammapada (ch. xx, 278), trans. F. Max Muller, quoted in *The Teachings of the Compassionate Buddha: Early discourses, the Dhammapada, and later basic writings,* ed. E. A. Burtt (New York: New American Library, 1955), 66.

5. Samyutta Nikaya (I 62).

6. This presentation of the *paticca-samuppada* contains some unorthodox elements. One of these is the inclusion, among the traditional twelve terms, of their own usually superimposed division into three consecutive life episodes. Another change is the exclusion from the chain of the term *tanha* ("desire"). The reason for excluding *tanha* is that, as the *cause* of suffering (and I am more inclined to trust the Four Noble Truths than the *paticca-samuppada), tanha* could not occupy such a derivative position. Instead, I assume that the *paticca-samuppada* (for the most part) is simply an analysis and elaboration of *tanha,* so that the term itself could not occur in its own expansion. The active agent of causality remains *sankhara* (but which I have translated as "configurations"). The condition for these "configurations" is *avijja* (ignorance), itself the legacy of the first life episode or past generation. The objects of *sankhara* are three other members of the *khandha* or five modes: bodily form or *rupa,* its internal environment or *vedana* ("expression"), and its contact with the external environment or *sanna* ("impression"). The fifth *khandha, vinnana* or "entrancement", follows as the next distinct causal link in the chain, and as the first-level sphere of consciousness. The second and third-level spheres of consciousness come next as *nama-rupa* ("conceptualization") and *salayatana* ("sentience"), respectively. The objects of *salayatana* ("sentience") are others like ourselves—the present generation (or second life episode). *Phassa* ("communication") is the first in an ever increasing intensification of *association.* It feeds into *upadana* (clinging), which bears fruit in *bhavana* ("birthright"). The projection of this latter into a future generation as *jati* ("the third life episode") leads to *dukkha* ("constraint").

The only goal of the impulse received from the previous life episode is self-reproduction. But it must first employ a series of

ESSAY II

psycho-physiological-behavioral forms, transmuting itself many times over, before it is able to replicate itself. It is at the phase of sentience that the element of sensuality, often associated with *tanha,* comes into play. But the causality of the *paticca-samuppada* is an internal or self-contained one. It does not receive any further causal input along the chain (as having object-sensations play an autonomous role implies), but rather *impacts* its inherent causality at each phase of the chain. But as hinted at above, the *paticca-samuppada* should probably be thought of as simply the intricacies of a single causal agency, *tanha* ("compulsion"), otherwise the statement of the second Truth seems irrelevant, there being other equally volitional conditions (phases of the chain) supporting *dukkha.* But not only is there no new causal input other than the initial one; neither can the causality be broken once begun: the fruits of karma must always be reaped. The rebirth impulse also does not simply travel through the various stages of the *paticca-samuppada* and then out the far end extinguishing itself, but persists for great durations at all stages of the chain. This is because amelioration can never occur along this negative axis of karma, but only along the positive axis of the Eightfold Way leading to the end of constraint. The negative axis is the natural home of karma, where the rebirth impulse, once received, is trapped and either succeeds in reproducing itself, or as a result of the fulfillment of the positive axis of the Eightfold Way, ceases.

Of course, we take such liberties with the traditional formulation because our goal is to reconstruct as original (or, it might be argued, as fundamental) a dharma as possible from the most nondoctrinal portions of the *Tripitaka.* The reader will more fully appreciate these adjustments when he/she is presented further along in the text with a real-life (rather than a textual) understanding of what rebirth actually is, and was; a discovery which provides my own justification for reassessing the traditional arrangement.

7. Majjhima Nikaya (I no. 36), in *The Middle Length Discourses of the Buddha: A New Translation of the Majjhima Nikaya,* trans. Bhikkhu Nanamoli and Bhikkhu Bodhi (Boston: Wisdom Publications, 1985), 337.

138

ESSAY II

8. Samyutta Nikaya (V 420–1), in E. A. Burtt's *The Teachings of the Compassionate Buddha,* 29.

9. Majjhima Nikaya (I no. 36), in Bhikkhu Nanamoli and Bhikkhu Bodhi's *The Middle Length Discourses of the Buddha,* 340.

10. *ibid.,* (I no. 8), 125.

11. Majjhima Nikaya (I no. 28), from "The Word of the Buddha," trans. Nyanatiloka. Quoted in *A Buddhist Bible,* comp. Dwight Goddard (New York: E. P. Dutton, 1966; reprint, Boston: Beacon Press, 1970), 26.

12. Majjhima Nikaya (III no. 140), in Nyanatiloka's *The Word of the Buddha* (Kandy, Sri Lanka: Buddhist Publication Society, 1981), 89.

13. Sutta Nipata (650), in *The Rhinoceros Horn and other early Buddhist poems: Sutta Nipata,* trans. K. R. Norman (London: Pali Text Society, 1985), 107.

14. Majjhima Nikaya (I no. 22), in Dwight Goddard's *A Buddhist Bible,* 36.

15. Samyutta Nikaya (III 150).

16. Samyutta Nikaya (III 188–9).

17. Digha Nikaya (I 99), in *Thus Have I Heard: The Long Discourses of the Buddha,* trans. Maurice Walshe (London: Wisdom Publications, 1987), 118.

18. Narasu, "The Historic Buddha," in Dwight Goddard's *A Buddhist Bible,* 10.

19. Sutta Nipata (648–649), in K. R. Norman's *The Rhinoceros Horn and other early Buddhist poems,* 107.

20. Majjhima Nikaya (I no. 28), in Dwight Goddard's *A Buddhist Bible,* 25.

21. Udana (ch. viii, 3), in *ibid.,* 32–33.

22. Digha Nikaya (I 99–100), in Maurice Walshe's *The Long Discourses of the Buddha,* 119.

23. Chandogya Upanishad (Book V, ch. iii, 7), in *The Wisdom of the Forest,* trans. Geoffrey Parrinder (New York: New Directions, 1976), 9–10, 16, 58. See Also *Hindu Scriptures,* trans. R. C. Zaehner (London: J. M. Dent & Sons, 1966), 110–13.

ESSAY II

24. Majjhima Nikaya (I no. 72), in Dwight Goddard's *A Buddhist Bible,* 38.

25. Katha Upanishad (Book II, 25), in *The Upanishads, Breath of the Eternal,* trans. Swami Prabhavananda and Frederick Manchester (New York: New American Library, Mentor, 1957), 19.

26. Sutta Nipata (5–6), in K. R. Norman's *The Rhinoceros Horn and other early Buddhist poems,* 1.

27. Samyutta Nikaya (ch. xxxv, no. 145). In our *historical* Buddhism "old karma" is the *parents'* volition (karma) in choosing one another for spouses and in choosing to have a child.

28. Sutta Nipata (651–654), in K. R. Norman's *The Rhinoceros Horn and other early Buddhist poems,* 107–108.

29. Samyutta Nikaya (III 77–78), in *An Anthology from the Samyutta Nikaya: Part I–III,* Part I trans. John Ireland (Kandi, Sri Lanka: Buddhist Publication Society, 1981), 41.

30. Samyutta Nikaya (ch. xxxv, no. 53), in *ibid.,* 58–59.

31. *See* Mathieu Boisvert, *The Five Aggregates: Understanding Theravada Psychology and Soteriology* (Waterloo, Ontario: Wilfrid Laurier University Press for the Canadian Corporation for Studies in Religion), 2–3.

32. Majjhima Nikaya (I 40–6), trans. Michael Carithers. Quoted in *The Buddha,* Past Masters, Michael Carithers (Oxford: Oxford Univ. Press, 1983), 35

33. Anguttara Nikaya (III 5), in *The Buddha's Path to Deliverance,* trans. Nyanatiloka (Kandy, Sri Lanka: Buddhist Publication Society, 1982), 33.

34. Digha Nikaya (I 123), in *Dialogues of the Buddha,* trans. T. W. and C. A. F. Rhys Davids. Quoted in *The Wisdom of the Early Buddhists,* comp. Geoffrey Parrinder (New York: New Directions, 1977), 41.

ESSAY III

1. *Samyutta Nikaya* (II 29).
2. The three quoted phrases of this paragraph are from the

ESSAY III

Dhammapada (ch. xx, 278, 279, 280). I have chosen to render the Pali word **dhamma** by the English 'tradition,' a meaning closer to the Hindu usage. I think this to be justified because the Hindu usage remained in the social context (of castes) which the Buddha confronted, and from which the (metaphysical) *Abhidhamma* scholars became alienated. The Mahayana, also, had disagreed with the *Abhidhamma's* metaphysical extension of the dharma, but did not, of course, revert to the earliest social context as I have done. (Even though the first of these three statements establishes the reality of mortality, and so would seem to exclude the possibility of a trans-generational entity, the last statement is still necessary because "tradition" outlives mortality.)

3. *Samyutta Nikaya* (I 134–5). The four questions are asked by Mara (the Evil One) to a nun, by the name of Vajira, doing her meditations at the foot of a tree. Her response takes up the rest of the quote.

4. *ibid.* (I 9).

5. *Visuddhi Magga* (ch. xvi, 513), quoted in Nyanatiloka's *The Word of the Buddha* (Kandy, Sri Lanka: Buddhist Publication Society, 1981), 40. The "doer," of course, referred to blood-identity, so pervasive and suffocating in ancient India—so completely definitive of the individual—that when it was given up it seemed the 'person' had ceased to exist! The Buddha himself gives evidence (M II no. 84) that the old standard whereby a person was punished for a crime according to his estate (or blood-) identity, was now seriously challenged. The new reality saw a person punished according to the crime; so as far as the legal system was concerned, the 'person' did not exist at all, only his crime or action. This quoted line is one of a verse quatrain which also asserts (1) the nonexistence of the 'person' who suffers (is constrained), (2) who enters nirvana, and (3) who travels the Path. These expressed the fact that (3) a blood-identity was incompatible with practice of the Buddha's dharma; (2) that it had to be abandoned to achieve the goal of practice; and (1) that wrongdoing was treated irrespective of estate identity—a wronged commoner (Vaisya), or possibly even a Sudra, could now expect some sort of

ESSAY III

hearing against an accused Kshatriya or Brahman. But even in the Buddha's definition of suffering as constraint (the attachment to the five modes) the ones who were actually the most constrained of all, because so obsessed were they with blood purity, were the birthright Brahmans—though supposedly closer to liberation than anyone else. (*see also* Carithers, *The Buddha,* p. 16.)

6. *Samyutta Nikaya* (II 180).

7. *ibid.* (III 34).

8. *ibid.* (III 21). It is the view of impermanence as a positive factor which I have tried to maintain in this particular rendering. Of the three characteristics of reality—*anicca, anatta* and *dukkha*—only the first two—impermanence and nonidentity—are absolute. The third, constraint, ceases with the realization of nirvana. So that impermanence, continuing to exist with the attainment of nirvana, could not be a source of *dukkha.* Instead, that is the function of rebirth. As the First Truth makes clear, rebirth is the first occurrence of *dukkha,* and it is within rebirth (and not simply birth) that all of the life-process is constrained in old age, sickness, death, etc. And in fact, *rebirth* posits continuity, and so is antithetical to impermanence. Thus the Buddha makes use of the "perceiving of impermanence" as a valuable 'practice' against rebirth and *dukkha* (S ch. xxii 102).

9. *ibid.* (III 68).

10. *Theragatha,* in *Psalms of the Early Buddhists,* ed. C. A. F. Rhys Davids (London: Pali Text Society, 1909). Quoted in E. A. Burtt's *The Teachings of the Compassionate Buddha,* 75.

11. Ayn Rand, *Anthem* (New York: Penguin-Signet), 119.

12. *Digha Nikaya* (II 90).

Glossary of terms

adicca—the sun; used in an epithet of the Buddha "kinsman of the *adicca.*"

anatta—literally nonidentity; the Buddha's doctrine of nonidentity, the nonidentification with the five modes (which make up the personality).

atman ("identity," Sanskrit)—originally having as innate potential the universal identity of Brahma, by the time of the Buddha designating exclusively the blood-identities of estate and clan, expressed in the five modes.

ariya loka (Pali)—the Aryan world.

Aryan (Pali *ariya*)—aristocrat; noble.

bhikku—monk

Brahma—the universal identity attained by a Brahman.

dharma (Pali *dhamma*)—the word the Buddha used and Buddhists still use for the doctrine and practice of Buddhism.

dukkha—constraint; suffering.

Mara (literally "murderer," "death")—the god of death, the great Tempter, (the personification of) the major obstacle in the way of nirvana.

modes or "aggregates," the five (Pali *khandha,* Sanskrit *skandha*)—commonly translated as "body, feeling, perception, mental formations and consciousness," they are rendered here, respectively, as bodily form, expression, impression, configurations and entrancement.

moksha—release from rebirth and constraint.

nirvana (Pali *nibbana*)—the breaking or sundering of constraint; the goal of the dharma.

rebirth or reincarnation—the compulsive retention of "blood" or racial type.

samsara—the cycle of rebirths; upholding an unchanging transgenerational identity as existing within one's genealogy.

Sonadanda—a Brahman who, appreciating the Buddha's message, told the Buddha he would pay respect to him in code so he, Sonadanda, would not lose his respect among other Brahmans (D I no. 4).

Tathagata ("thus traveled")—a term by which the Buddha referred to himself.

upadana ("clinging")—that relationship (to the five modes) which generates constraint.

Bibliography

ESSAY I

Carithers, Michael. *The Buddha,* Past Masters. Oxford and New York: Oxford University Press, 1983.

Garvey, Amy Jacques, ed. *The Philosophy and Opinions of Marcus Garvey.* New York: Arno Press, 1968–'69. Reprint, New York: Atheneum, 1980.

Hamner, Robert D., ed. *Critical Perspectives on V. S. Naipaul.* Washington, D.C.: Three Continents Press, 1977.

Holcomb, Bonnie K. and Sisai Ibssa. *The Invention of Ethiopia: The Making of a Dependent Colonial State in Northeast Africa.* Trenton, New Jersey: Red Sea Press, 1990.

Johnson, Andrew. "The Gungadin of Caribbean Literature." *Trinidad Express,* March 7th, 1982.

Naipaul, V. S. *The Mimic Men.* London: André Deutsch. 1967. Reprint, Harmondsworth, England: Penguin Books, 1969.

———. *Guerrillas.* New York: Alfred A. Knopf. 1975. Reprint, New York: Vintage International, 1990.

———. *A Bend in the River.* New York: Alfred A. Knopf. 1979. Reprint, New York: Vintage International, 1989.

———. *Finding the Center.* London: André Deutsch. 1984. Reprint, Harmondsworth, England: Penguin Books, 1985.

———. Interview by Ian Hamilton, "Without a Place," *Times Literary Supplement,* 30 July 1971, 897. Quoted in John Thieme, *A Critical View on V. S. Naipaul's "The Mimic Men"* (London: Collins, 1985), 27–28.

———. "A Plea for Rationality." *Indians in the Caribbean.* Ed. I. J. Bahadur Singh. New Delhi: Sterling, 1987.

Walcott, Derek. *In A Green Night.* London: Jonathan Cape, 1962.

———. *Collected Poems 1948–1984.* New York: The Noonday Press, 1986.

———. *Omeros.* New York: The Noonday Press, 1990.

Bibliography

ESSAY II

Boisvert, Mathieu. *The Five Aggregates: Understanding Theravada Psychology and Soteriology.* Waterloo, Ontario: Wilfrid Laurier University Press for the Canadian Corporation for Studies in Religion, 1995.

Burtt, E. A., ed. *The Teachings of the Compassionate Buddha: Early discourses, the Dhammapada, and later basic writings.* New York: New American Library, 1955.

Carithers, Michael. *The Buddha,* Past Masters. Oxford and New York: Oxford University Press, 1983.

Conze, Edward, trans. *Buddhist Scriptures.* Harmondsworth, England: Penguin Books, 1959.

Goddard, Dwight, comp. *A Buddhist Bible.* New York: E. P. Dutton. 1938, 1966. Reprint, with an introduction by Huston Smith, Boston: Beacon Press, 1970.

Ireland, John, et. al. *An Anthology from the Samyutta Nikaya: Part I–III.* Part I, 1981, trans. John Ireland; Part II, 1972, trans. Bhikkhu Nanananda; Part III, 1985, trans. M. O' C. Walshe. Kandi, Sri Lanka: Buddhist Publication Society.

Mascaró, Juan, trans. *The Dhammapada.* Harmondsworth, England: Penguin Books, 1973.

Mizuno, Kogen. *The Beginnings of Buddhism.* Trans. Richard L. Gage. Tokyo: Kosei Publishing, 1980.

Nanamoli, Bhikkhu and Bhikkhu Bodhi. *The Middle Length Discourses of the Buddha: A New Translation of the Majjhima Nikaya.* Boston: Wisdom Publications, 1985.

Narasu. "The Historic Buddha" in *A Buddhist Bible.* Comp. Dwight Goddard. Boston: Beacon Press, 1970.

Norman, K. R. *The Rhinoceros Horn and other early Buddhist poems: Sutta Nipata.* London: The Pali Text Society, 1985.

Nyanatiloka. *Buddhist Dictionary: Manual of Buddhist Terms and Doctrines.* Kandy, Sri Lanka: Buddhist Publication Society, 1980.

———. *The Word of the Buddha.* Kandy, Sri Lanka: Buddhist Publication Society, 1981.

———. *The Buddha's Path to Deliverance.* Kandy, Sri Lanka: Buddhist Publication Society, 1982.

Parrinder, Geoffrey, comp. *The Wisdom of the Early Buddhists.* New

146

York: New Directions, 1977.

————. *The Wisdom of the Forest: Selections from the Hindu Upanishads.* New York: New Directions, 1976.

Pe Maung Tin. *The Path of Purity: Being a Translation of Buddhaghosa's Visuddhimagga.* London: The Pali Text Society, 1975.

Prabhavananda, Swami and Frederick Manchester. *The Upanishads, Breath of the Eternal.* New York: New American Library, Mentor, 1957.

Rahula, Walpola. *What the Buddha Taught.* New York: Grove Weidenfeld, 1974.

Schloegel, I. *The Zen Teachings of Rinzai,* 43. Boulder: Shambala Publications, 1976. Quoted in Judith Blackstone & Zoran Josipovic, illustrated by Naomi Rosenblatt, *Zen for Beginners* (London: Writers and Readers Documentary Comic Books & Unwin Paperbacks, 1986), 92.

Thich Nhat Hanh. *The Miracle of Mindfulness: A Manual on Meditation.* Trans. Mobi Ho. Boston: Beacon Press, 1975.

Walshe, Maurice. *Thus Have I Heard: The Long Discourses of the Buddha (Digha Nikaya).* London: Wisdom Publications, 1987.

Zaehner, R. C. *Hindu Scriptures.* London: J. M. Dent & Sons; Rutland: Charles E. Tuttle Co. Rutland, Vermont, 1966.

Index

ESSAY II

ESSAY III

Index of first lines
(paragraph group number, page number)

The positive and the negative are poles apart. To find one is (7, 100)
The world of identity is not a world of color. It is a bleak (80, 133)
The ravening appetite of the black beast will goad it on, my (33, 111)
Their crying drove you to your knees in that conceited (55, 120)
Their identity is a sore in other men's eyes, but your own (47, 116)
There is nothing above History, and nothing beyond. It is (84, 134)
There is no inalienable stain in my blood. Do not ask how (26, 108)
There is so much nonexistence in the world. So many things (81, 133)
These five modes do not fit your color scheme. Yet you (25, 107)
Those who cannot wholly embrace the energies of the body (12, 103)
Though no one could have known, through this endless (44, 114)
Thus traveled, O sacred self, do not give a lodging to the (56, 120)
Turn away from the scornful ones who say, "Look! They (76, 131)

We are not asking anyone's permission to claim our heritage. (41, 114)
We were *born* in History. Ages ago, on that other isle, we (36, 112)
When the springtime approaches near, there is the feeling of (3, 98)
Where did you get that garage-sale atman from, my boy, that (60, 123)

Yet whether they come from the jungles of the Congo or the (32, 111)
You accuse the fairer ones of disowning the darker ones, as (24, 107)
You *must* allow the hypocrites to go their sullen ways. You (68, 127)
You reserve nobility for yourselves and deny it to others, as (27, 108)
You were right to be ashamed, my mother, right to be (20, 106)